T5-CQD-786

do-it-yourself do-it-yourself
do-it-yourself do-it-yourself
do-it-yourself do-it-yourself
do-it-yourself do-it-yourself
do-it-yourself do-it-yourself
do-it-yourself do-it-yourself
do-it-yourself do-it-yourself
do-it-yourself do-it-yourself
do-it-yourself do-it-yourself
do-it-yourself do-it-yourself
do-it-yourself do-it-yourself
do-it-yourself do-it-yourself
do-it-yourself do-it-yourself
do-it-yourself do-it-yourself
do-it-yourself do-it-yourself
do-it-yourself do-it-yourself
do-it-yourself do-it-yourself
do-it-yourself do-it-yourself
do-it-yourself do-it-yourself
do-it-yourself do-it-yourself
do-it-yourself do-it-yourself
do-it-yourself do-it-yourself
do-it-yourself do-it-yourself
do-it-yourself do-it-yourself
do-it-yourself do-it-yourself
do-it-yourself do-it-yourself
do-it-yourself do-it-yourself
do-it-yourself do-it-yourself
do-it-yourself do-it-yourself
do-it-yourself do-it-yourself
do-it-yourself do-it-yourself
do-it-yourself do-it-yourself
do-it-yourself do-it-yourself
do-it-yourself do-it-yourself
do-it-yourself do-it-yourself
do-it-yourself do-it-yourself
do-it-yourself do-it-yourself
do-it-yourself do-it-yourself
do-it-yourself do-it-yourself
do-it-yourself do-it-yourself
do-it-yourself do-it-yourself
do-it-yourself do-it-yourself
do-it-yourself do-it-yourself
do-it-yourself do-it-yourself
do-it-yourself do-it-yourself
do-it-yourself do-it-yourself
do-it-yourself do-it-yourself
do-it-yourself do-it-yourself
do-it-yourself do-it-yourself
do-it-yourself do-it-yourself
do-it-yourself do-it-yourself
do-it-yourself do-it-yourself

PAINTING, PANELING, AND WALLPAPERING

do-it-yourself do-it-yourself
do-it-yourself do-it-yourself
do-it-yourself do-it-yourself
do-it-yourself do-it-yourself
do-it-yourself do-it-yourself
do-it-yourself do-it-yourself
do-it-yourself do-it-yourself
do-it-yourself do-it-yourself
do-it-yourself do-it-yourself
do-it-yourself do-it-yourself
do-it-yourself do-it-yourself
do-it-yourself do-it-yourself
do-it-yourself do-it-yourself
do-it-yourself do-it-yourself
do-it-yourself do-it-yourself
do-it-yourself do-it-yourself
do-it-yourself do-it-yourself
do-it-yourself do-it-yourself
do-it-yourself do-it-yourself
do-it-yourself do-it-yourself
do-it-yourself do-it-yourself
do-it-yourself do-it-yourself
do-it-yourself do-it-yourself
do-it-yourself do-it-yourself
do-it-yourself do-it-yourself
do-it-yourself do-it-yourself
do-it-yourself do-it-yourself
do-it-yourself do-it-yourself
do-it-yourself do-it-yourself
do-it-yourself do-it-yourself
do-it-yourself do-it-yourself
do-it-yourself do-it-yourself
do-it-yourself do-it-yourself
do-it-yourself do-it-yourself
do-it-yourself do-it-yourself
do-it-yourself do-it-yourself
do-it-yourself do-it-yourself
do-it-yourself do-it-yourself
do-it-yourself do-it-yourself
do-it-yourself do-it-yourself
do-it-yourself do-it-yourself
do-it-yourself do-it-yourself
do-it-yourself do-it-yourself
do-it-yourself do-it-yourself

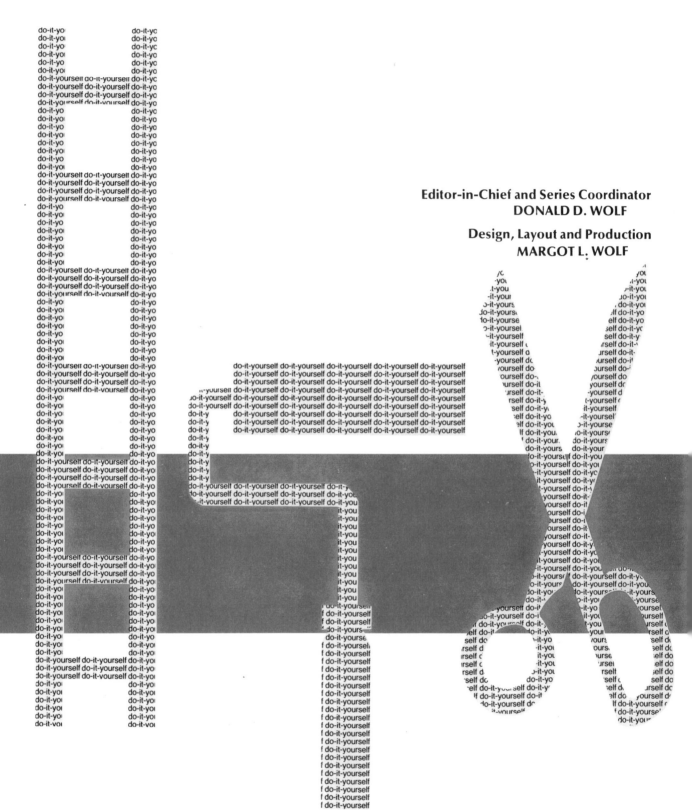

Editor-in-Chief and Series Coordinator
DONALD D. WOLF

Design, Layout and Production
MARGOT L. WOLF

ADVENTURES IN HOME REPAIR SERIES

PAINTING, PANELING, AND WALLPAPERING

Written by
DICK DEMSKE

Illustrated by
JAMES E. BARRY

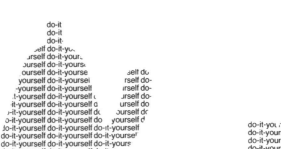

Consolidated Book Publishers

NEW YORK • CHICAGO

Introduction

Painting is the revered granddaddy of all modern-day do-it-yourself chores, and the one on which so many men and women have cut their home handyperson teeth. For the efforts you put into a paint job, the rewards—a bright, fresh appearance in a room or on an entire house—are satisfying and readily apparent (more so than, say, a plumbing repair that is hidden out of sight where you can't show it off to your neighbors). It is also a job that an amateur—a careful one—can do with professional-appearing results. But, like anything else, there are right ways and wrong ways to paint, and right ways are definitely better. Knowing what paint to use and how to apply it properly might not make you a rival to Michelangelo, but it will certainly produce a job of which you can be proud.

There is more than one way to skin a wall. Wallpaper (a term that applies to many materials in addition to paper) has regained its former position of popularity after a couple of decades in decorator's limbo. The reason: a profusion of very attractive patterns and greatly simplified methods of application. And paneling, primarily developed as a do-it-yourselfer's product, continues to be a favorite, available in a seemingly endless variety of designs in addition to the traditional wood grains.

However you choose to finish your walls—with paint, paper, or paneling—there are do's and don'ts that should be observed. You should thoroughly familiarize yourself with the correct procedures for the various operations, as outlined in these pages. Of course, not everyone is cut out to be a do-it-yourselfer; some of us can't pick up a paintbrush without becoming menaces to ourselves and all around us. But most of the jobs described herein are relatively easy. To help you determine whether they fall within your capabilities, we have consulted with professional painters, paperhangers, and carpenters, and with manufacturers of the various products, to rate the degree of difficulty of each operation. Those marked ● should pose no problems for the reasonably dexterous handyperson. ▲ jobs require a bit more skill and experience, but are still well within the do-it-yourselfer's domain. A ▇ rating means that only a person with advanced skills and knowledge should tackle the project.

Every effort has been made to ensure the accuracy, reliability, and up-to-dateness of the information and instructions in this book. We are not infallible, however—and neither are you. We cannot guarantee that there are no human or typographical errors herein, nor can we guarantee that you will not err in following our directions. We only hope that if this happens, it will not lessen the feeling of satisfaction you receive from doing-it-yourself.

DONALD D. WOLF

Contents

1

Color and How to Use It

APPEARANCE is usually the primary motivation for painting, and it's true that a fresh paint job on the inside or outside of a house is the easiest way to improve its looks. Protection is also important, particularly on the home's exterior. Where bare wood or metal are exposed to the weather, you can expect deterioration and decay, as well as a shabby appearance. The most economical way to provide the necessary protection is with a coat of paint. A good paint job is not cheap, but it is a worthwhile investment. A first-class paint job pays off in better looks over longer life, resulting in less cost per year.

When should you paint? Indoors, it doesn't make much difference. Many people like to brighten up their homes in the late fall in preparation for the holiday season. Others devote the whole winter to a room-by-room rejuvenation of the home. Midsummer is the only time we don't recommend—those hot days should be reserved for cooler activities. The same goes for exterior painting—not only would the hot sun cause discomfort, but also most paints cannot be satisfactorily applied in such heat. Of course, you won't paint outdoors in very cold weather, either. Spring is the favorite time for exterior painting, but early in the fall is just as good, especially if there are areas on your home that are down to bare wood. Such areas should at least be touched up, if you do not plan on painting the whole house at this time. It's a Band-Aid approach, but better than nothing.

Should you do it yourself? The question can be answered only by you, since you must realistically assess your own capabilities in the light of the job to be done. If you're afraid of heights, stay away from exterior painting above the first story. If you have a distaste for such time-consuming jobs as scraping, burning, and calking, stick to interior painting, where these measures are not required. But if you have the time and patience, you can do a highly satisfactory and satisfying job on your home. And, perhaps more important, you will be able to save from $150 to $500 on the interior, and from $350 to $1,000 on the exterior by doing the job yourself.

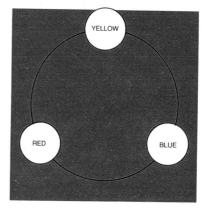

Color wheel.

Primary colors.

THE COLOR SCHEME

The basic factor in color harmony is the color wheel. An understanding of the fundamental elements of color, as illustrated by the color wheel, is very helpful in planning successful decorating schemes.

The primary colors are yellow, red, and blue. Secondary colors are combinations of the primary colors on either side. The wheel is completed by combining the primary and secondary colors and forming a third group, called the tertiary or intermediate colors.

Colors have certain psychological effects upon human beings, and these effects may be broken down into two groups. Warm colors are happy, stimulating, bright, spirited. These colors are generally on the left side of the color wheel, ranging from yellow to red. Cool colors are those that are quiet, soothing, restful, and placid. These colors are more on the right side of the wheel—mainly greens and blues.

As in music, harmony in color means the pleasant association of one tone with another. Interior decoration leans heavily upon the skillful use of these associations. There are many types of color harmony.

Monochromatic harmony is the simplest, and probably the most overlooked, form of color harmony. It is simply the use of different intensities of the same color, such as green, light green, and dark green. Tints and shades of the same color are formed by adding white or black to the original hue. This type of harmony creates an impression of sophistication by combining quiet and subdued contrast.

Analogous harmony uses colors that are next to each other on the color wheel. Two to four colors in sequence may be used. Softness and delicacy are the result.

Complementary harmony is one of the easiest ways to create a lively color scheme. Simply use the two colors that are exact opposites on the color wheel.

Split-complementary harmony gives more variety. Determine which will be your basic color, find its true complement, then use either or both adjacent colors.

Double-complementary harmony splits both ends of the true complements, and gets two sets of complements.

Mutual complements as a color scheme utilizes five analogous colors (next to each other on the color wheel). The true complement of the middle color of this group is then used for contrast. Color planning of this type frequently achieves a bright, lively effect, with the complement of the middle color providing a dramatic contrast.

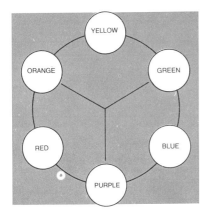

Secondary colors.

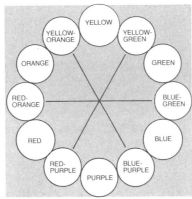

Tertiary colors.

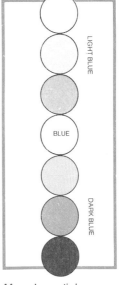

Monochromatic harmony.

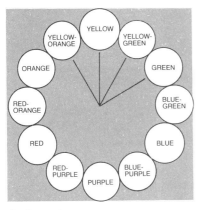

Analogous harmony.

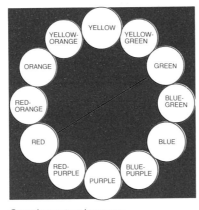

Complementary harmony.

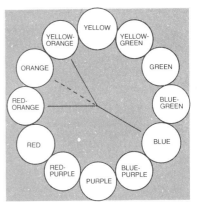

Split-complementary harmony.

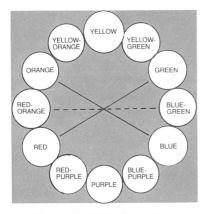

Double-complementary harmony.

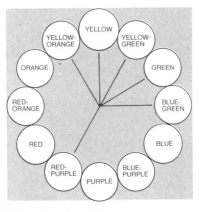

Mutual complements.

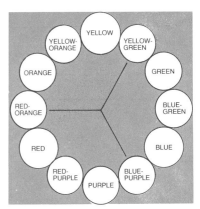

Triad harmony.

Color and How to Use It • Chapter 1

Triad harmony is one of the most common and basic color schemes, utilizing three colors on the wheel equidistant from each other.

Obviously, there are many different ways to decorate a home—even further combinations of the color schemes discussed above. The important factors are to plan some sort of pattern, and to avoid the extremes of monotony and overdiversity.

COLOR CAMOUFLAGE

The right paint can have a magic effect in emphasizing the good points and hiding the defects of a home. Light colors reflect and tend to create a cheerful atmosphere—they are effective in making small rooms seem larger. Dark colors absorb light and, when used extensively on large surfaces, tend to be depressing. They can be used to make a large, well-lighted room seem smaller and more intimate. If a ceiling is too high, painting it a dark color may give a better sense of proportion to the room. Bright colors attract the eye and may be employed to distract attention from an unattractive feature—they may also, if improperly used, become irritating. Warm colors—reds, oranges, yellows—convey a cozy feeling and are stimulating, whereas the cool colors—blues, greens, violets—are relaxing and cooling.

Light Reflectance of Various Colors

You may wish to make the most of the natural and artificial light within a room (such as a kitchen), or you may want to soften the glare that sometimes enters through large glass areas (such as a living room with southern exposure). Dark colors absorb light, whereas light colors reflect it, as indicated by this chart.

White	80%
Light ivory	71%
Apricot-beige	66%
Lemon yellow	65%
Ivory	59%
Light buff	56%
Peach	53%
Salmon	53%
Pale apple green	51%
Medium gray	43%
Light green	41%
Pale blue	41%
Deep rose	12%
Dark green	9%

Red is stimulating. It makes a room look smaller and dominates in large doses, but it may provide just the excitement you are looking for. Green has the opposite effect; it is smooth and tranquil. Yellow is cheerful, blue is soothing, purple is subduing and somewhat regal. White, gray, brown, and beige are neutral colors that make fine backgrounds but can be dull when used as the principal decorating schemes. These neutral colors have found a certain popularity among modern designers, however.

Decide which features of the room you feel should be accented, which you wish to minimize. A fireplace or some other feature of interest might be made the focal point of the decorating scheme; accent it by painting the surrounding wall a contrasting color. A long, narrow room may take on seemingly improved proportions if one of the end walls is painted a darker hue than the

Painting a too-high ceiling in a darker color makes room appear lower.

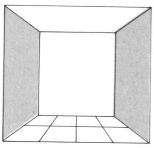 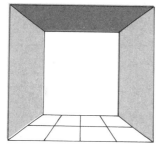

other walls, visually drawing it closer to the center of the room. Painting the walls and woodwork the same color gives a sense of spaciousness and trimness—painting the woodwork in an accenting color can complement the walls and point up some special characteristic.

A room should also be considered in terms of its function as well as its relation to neighboring rooms. An entryway, for example, should be painted in friendly, inviting tones, and in tones that will blend naturally with those of the living areas into which it leads the visitor. If you entertain formally, or enjoy dining by candlelight, dining-room colors should help to enhance the moods that are sought. And, of course, the colors on a room's walls must harmonize with the furniture and accessories of that room. If you proudly display bright

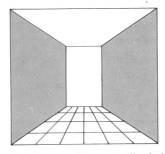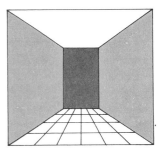

Painting one of the end walls of a long, narrow room in a darker color improves its appearance.

modern paintings on your walls, determine what wall colors will best show off the pictures without distracting attention from them. Often, a favorite drapery material or a cherished couch or other piece of furniture is the key to the decorating scheme for a given room—and, ultimately, the color scheme for the entire home.

Color Do's and Don'ts

DO

• Remember that large areas of color emphasize the color. Choose a lighter shade for such areas.

• Use light colors in a small room to increase apparent size.

• Emphasize reds and yellows in windowless rooms.

• Make use of horizontal and vertical lines for giving visual balance to rooms with high or low ceilings.

• Use light colors in a small room to make it seem larger.

• Aim for a continuing color flow through your home—from room to room—using harmonious colors in adjoining areas.

• Paint the ceiling of a room in a deeper color than the walls if you want it to appear lower; paint it in a lighter shade for the opposite effect.

• Study color swatches in both daylight and nightlight. Colors often change under artificial lighting.

DON'T

• Use too large a pattern, or too much pattern in an area.

• Use equal proportions of colors; always use more of one color than another.

• Choose neutral or negative colors simply because they are safe and "mix well."

• Paint woodwork and trim of a small room in a color different from the background color, or the room will appear small and cluttered.

• Paint radiators, pipes, or similar projections in a color that contrasts with walls, or they will be emphasized.

• Use glossy paints on walls or ceilings of living areas, since the shiny surface creates undesirable glare.

Suggested Exterior Color Schemes

If your house has shutters, paint the trim the same color as the body of the house—or white. If not, use the trim colors suggested in the chart.

IF THE ROOF OF YOUR HOUSE IS	YOU CAN PAINT THE BODY	. . . and the trim or shutters and doors															
		Pink	Bright red	Red-orange	Tile red	Cream	Bright yellow	Light green	Dark green	Gray-green	Blue-green	Light blue	Dark blue	Blue-gray	Violet	Brown	White
GRAY	White	x	x	x	x	x	x	x	x	x	x	x	x	x	x		
	Gray	x	x	x	x		x	x	x	x	x	x	x	x	x		x
	Cream-yellow		x		x		x		x	x							x
	Pale green				x		x		x	x							x
	Dark green	x				x	x	x									x
	Putty			x	x					x			x	x		x	
	Dull red	x				x		x						x			x
GREEN	White	x	x	x	x	x	x	x	x	x	x	x	x	x	x	x	
	Gray			x		x	x	x									x
	Cream-yellow		x		x				x	x	x					x	x
	Pale green			x	x		x		x								x
	Dark green	x		x		x	x	x									x
	Beige				x				x	x	x		x	x			
	Brown	x				x	x	x									x
	Dull red					x		x		x							x
RED	White		x		x				x		x			x			
	Light gray		x		x				x								x
	Cream-yellow		x		x							x	x	x			
	Pale green		x		x												x
	Dull red					x		x		x	x						x
BROWN	White			x	x		x	x	x	x	x		x	x	x	x	
	Buff				x				x	x	x					x	
	Pink-beige				x				x	x						x	x
	Cream-yellow				x				x	x	x					x	
	Pale green								x	x						x	
	Brown			x		x	x										x
BLUE	White			x	x		x					x	x				
	Gray			x	x							x	x				x
	Cream-yellow			x	x								x	x			
	Blue			x		x	x					x					x

Exterior sleight of hand can also be accomplished by a coat of paint. A fresh, crisp appearance can give a formerly drab and tired-looking home a new lease on life—and a definite psychological lift to its inhabitants. But it can do even more than that—it can alter the entire physical appearance of the house.

Often, the roof color sets the tone for the rest of the house. If it is a neutral hue, the home can be brightened up by the use of a bolder, warm color such as red. Low homes can be made to look higher by emphasizing vertical lines with trim paint. Top-heavy, boxy structures benefit from color-accenting of horizontal lines such as fasciae and windowsills. Painting the upper story a darker color than the lower achieves the same effect. Split levels look better when they are not too "split." The different levels should usually be the same color. Large homes, particularly if they are well landscaped, lend themselves better to the cooler hues of the spectrum. Many vintage homes suffer from the visual weight of a profusion of gables and other projections. These should be camouflaged by painting them to match their surroundings, so that there is at least a suggestion of harmony and continuity in the home's lines.

Color is highly personal. Certain rules and color schemes can be suggested, but don't be afraid to use your own good taste and initiative. It's your house and your money. If it turns out to be a visual atrocity, you can always repaint. But chances are good that, with a little forethought and the careful selection of colors, a fresh coat of paint, both indoors and out, will do your home proud.

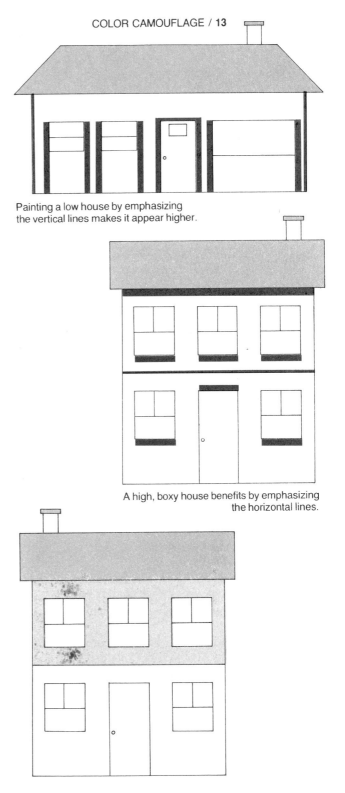

Painting a low house by emphasizing the vertical lines makes it appear higher.

A high, boxy house benefits by emphasizing the horizontal lines.

The same effect can be achieved by painting a high, boxy house in two colors.

2

Paint Selection

A SEEMINGLY bewildering array of paints is available—but don't be bewildered. Each type is formulated to do specific things or to act in a specific way. It is just a matter of deciding which one is best suited to the job you want it to do.

One type of paint that is never suitable is the bargain-basement special. The only thing you can be sure of with a cheap paint is that you will be doing the job over again long before you should have to. This is one area where a penny saved is wasted money—and time.

Some paints (and some applications) require the use of an undercoat first; others can be applied directly as a first, or final, coat. Manufacturers include their recommendations on the paint labels, and these should always be strictly followed. Doing it yourself doesn't necessarily mean doing it your way. Or you'll be doing it over.

EXTERIOR PAINTS

Several types of paint for house exteriors are available. Ideally, a white house paint should have a clean, highly reflective whiteness. It should remain clean and white at all times during the life of the coating.

The ideal paint should not be affected by moisture. It should be resistant to staining by rust and other residues of metal corrosion. It should also resist mildew and should not be discolored by industrial gases. The paint should wear away at an even rate, leaving a smooth adherent film, suitable for repainting after a reasonable number of years.

Although no house paint on the market has all of these desirable characteristics, many modern paints of high quality can be depended upon to provide excellent performance under most of these conditions. You should be aware of the climatic and atmospheric conditions to which house paints are subjected in your area. Through your paint dealer, you should determine the types of house paint that perform best under local conditions and the performance characteristics that are most important to your paint job.

No one type of house paint is "better" than another in every respect. Within each type, almost any quality of paint may be made, depending upon the grades of ingredients used, their relative proportions, and the care used in compounding the product. Regardless of type of paint selected, there will be greater assurance of satisfactory service if the particular paint was produced by a reputable manufacturer and sold through a reputable dealer. No type of paint formulation will guarantee a high-quality product; this can be insured only by the integrity of the maker.

Paints used on house siding are mostly based on linseed oil—that is, they have linseed oil "vehicles" to carry the pigment. These paints have a long history of satisfactory service. Many improvements have been made by modifying the linseed oils and by changing the pigmentation. Further, since no one paint can satisfy all requirements under different conditions, paints have been specialized to produce the best result for various use requirements.

For example, white paints may be self-cleaning—free-chalking—for use where siding covers the lower portion of a house; or they may be chalk-resistant for use where chalk rundown will mar brick or stone below the siding. This should be kept in mind when buying white house paint, since chalk rundown on masonry is unsightly. Another type of white paint is fume-resistant. It is used where industrial or other fumes may be present and could stain the paint. For warm, humid conditions in most latitudes, mildew-resistant paints are used to discourage mildew discoloration.

If the old paint is sound but dirty, a one-coat paint will give a gleaming new surface. Chalk-resistant, pastel-colored paints can be made from white one-coat paints. All pastel tints must be made with chalk-resistant or tint-based paints to avoid early fading. Dark-colored paints cannot be made from white paint; they are colored during manufacture. There are shingle and shake paints and clear finishes for houses sided · with shingles or shakes. The choice depends on whether or not the grain pattern of the wood is to remain visible. Clear finishes need refinishing more frequently than opaque paints, but they reveal the beauty of the wood.

All the paints mentioned above, except clear finishes, require a primer when new wood is painted. For repainting, the primer is necessary only if the old paint is in bad condition. The primer should be the one recommended for the topcoat selected.

Over the past decade or so, exterior paints have been developed in which the solvent for the vehicle is water, instead of turpentine or mineral spirits—the solvents used for linseed oil. The first of these water-thinned products were the so-called latex paints, which are emulsions of the vehicle in water. After the paint is applied, the emulsion coalesces, permitting the water to evaporate, leaving the vehicle and pigment. More recent are paints in which the linseed oil vehicle is in true water solution. The oil had to be altered to accomplish this, but such paints have the properties of both water and oil paints. The advantages of both the emulsion and the linseed-oil solution include ease of application, cleanup with water, good tint retention, and easy cleaning. Emulsion paints dry faster than do the solution paints. As repaints, emulsion paints may not adhere well to chalky surfaces. The procedure recommended by the manufacturer must be followed. It will likely call

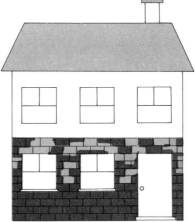

Self-cleaning paint may stain brick or other surfaces below it.

What To Use And Where
(Exterior Surfaces)

	House Paint (Oil or Oil-Alkyd)	Cement Powder Paint	Exterior Clear Finish	Aluminum Paint	Wood Stain	Roof Coating	Trim Paint	Porch and Deck Paint	Primer or Undercoater	Metal Primer	House Paint (Latex)	Water Repellent Preservative
MASONRY												
Asbestos Cement	X•								X		X	
Brick	X•	X	X						X		X	X
Cement & Cinder Block	X•	X	X						X		X	
Concrete/Masonry Porches												
And Floors								X			X	
Coal Tar Felt Roof						X						
Stucco	X•	X	X						X		X	
METAL												
Aluminum Windows	X•			X			X•			X	X•	
Steel Windows	X•			X•			X•			X	X•	
Metal Roof	X•									X	X•	
Metal Siding	X•			X•			X•			X	X•	
Copper Surfaces			X									
Galvanized Surfaces	X•			X•			X•			X	X•	
Iron Surfaces	X•			X•			X•			X	X•	
WOOD												
Clapboard	X•			X					X		X•	
Natural Wood Siding & Trim			X		X							
Shutters & Other Trim	X•						X•		X		X•	
Wood Frame Windows	X•			X			X•		X		X•	
Wood Porch Floor								X				
Wood Shingle Roof					X							X

X• Black dot indicates that a primer, sealer, or fill coat may be necessary before the finishing coat (unless surface has been previously finished).

for a primer for emulsion types to insure adhesion to chalky surfaces.

Moisture is the cause of much unsatisfactory paint service. Under certain conditions, the effects of moisture can be controlled best by using special blister-resistant paints. They may be oil- or water-base paints, and must be used as directed to obtain their maximum efficiency.

Exterior trim paints are used principally on wood trim, screen frames, shutters, and other small areas of the home. Dark, medium, and light greens are among the most popular colors. Good leveling or freedom from brush marks, rapid drying, high gloss, good color- and gloss-retention, one-coat hiding, and good durability are important properties of exterior trim paints. They are usually solvent-thinned.

Some paint manufacturers market special undercoats in a gray or other neutral color as a primer for the trim and dark-colored house paints. The regular primer for white and light-tinted house paints is also satisfactory as a primer for the dark-colored paints. This primer, generally white, may be tinted to a neutral gray or any other color with pastels in oil when used under dark-colored paints.

Exterior latex masonry paint is a standard paint for masonry. Cement-base paint may be used on nonglazed brick, stucco, cement, and cinder block. Rubber-base paint and aluminum paint with the proper vehicle may also be used.

Ordinary house or trim paints may be used for the finish coats on gutters, downspouts, and hardware or grilles. A specially recommended primer must be used on copper or galvanized steel. Use house paint, aluminum paint, or exterior enamel on steel or aluminum windows. Paint window screens with a special screen enamel.

Porch-and-deck paint may be used on both concrete and wood porches and steps. On wood, a primer coat is applied first. On concrete, an alkali-resistant primer is recommended. Rubber-base paints are excellent for use on concrete floors. Hard and glossy concrete surfaces must be etched or roughened first.

INTERIOR PAINTS

Many different kinds and formulations of paints and other finishes are available for interior use, and new ones frequently appear on the market. For a specific selection consult your paint dealer. Reputable dealers keep abreast of developments in the paint industry and stock the newest formulations. The usual interior paint job consists of painting wallboard or plaster walls and ceilings, woodwork, and wood windows and doors. For these surfaces you need to choose first between solvent-thinned paint (oil-based) and water-thinned paint (commonly called latex paint, but not necessarily latex), and then between a gloss, semigloss, or flat finish. (Enamels, which are made with a varnish or resin base instead of the usual linseed-oil vehicle, are included under the oil-paint grouping.)

Oil-based paints are very durable, are highly resistant to staining and damage, can withstand frequent scrubbings, and give good one-coat coverage. Many latex paints have similar properties. The main advantages of latex paint are easier application, faster drying, and simpler tool cleanup. The brushes, rollers, and other equipment can be easily cleaned with water.

Both oil-based and latex paints are available in gloss, semigloss, and flat finishes. Glossy finishes look shiny and clean easily. Flat finishes show dirt more readily but absorb light and thus reduce glare. Semigloss finishes have properties of both glossy and flat finishes.

Because enamel is durable and easy to clean, semigloss or gloss enamel is recommended for the walls of kitchens, bathrooms, and laundry rooms. For the walls of nurseries and playrooms, either oil-based or latex semigloss enamel paint is suggested. Flat paint is generally used for the walls of living rooms and other nonwork or nonplay rooms.

Ceilings are important as light-reflecting surfaces in most rooms, and they should have dull-surfaced coatings that reflect light evenly. In bathrooms and kitchens, however, semigloss finishes are generally more desirable because of their washability.

What To Use And Where
(Interior Surfaces)

Surface	Flat Enamel	Semigloss Enamel	Gloss Enamel	Interior Varnish	Shellac-Lacquer	Wax (Liquid or Paste)	Wax (Emulsion)	Stain	Wood Sealer	Floor Varnish	Floor Paint or Enamel	Aluminum Paint	Sealer or Undercoater	Metal Primer	Latex (Wall) Flat	Latex Gloss & Semigloss
MASONRY																
Asphalt Tile							X									
Concrete Floors						X•	X•	X			X				X	
Kitchen & Bathroom Walls		X•	X•										X			X•
Linoleum							X									
New Masonry	X•	X•											X		X	X•
Old Masonry	X	X										X	X		X	X•
Plaster Walls & Ceiling	X•	X•											X		X	X•
Vinyl & Rubber Tile Floors						X	X									
Wall Board	X•	X•											X		X	X•
METAL																
Aluminum Windows	X•	X•										X		X	X•	X•
Heating Ducts	X•	X•										X		X	X•	X•
Radiators & Heating Pipes	X•	X•										X		X	X•	X•
Steel Cabinets	X•	X•												X		X•
Steel Windows	X•	X•										X		X	X•	X•
WOOD																
Floors				X	X	X•	X•	X	X•	X•						
Paneling	X•	X•		X	X	X		X	X						X•	X•
Stair Risers	X•	X•		X	X			X	X							X•
Stair Treads				X				X	X	X	X					
Trim	X•	X•		X	X	X		X					X		X•	X•
Window Sills				X												

X• Black dot indicates that a primer or sealer may be necessary before the finishing coat (unless surface has been previously finished).

Plaster and wallboard ceilings can be coated with flat oil paints or paints of semigloss, emulsion, or rubber-base types. If the ceiling has not been previously painted, a primer should be applied before flat or semigloss paint. On acoustic tile, use flat paint, thinned in accordance with the manufacturer's recommendation. Woodwork that is new and is to be given an opaque coating requires an undercoat. For a finishing coat, you can use semigloss, enamel, or flat oil paint. Flat oil paints are easily finger-marked and are unsatisfactory for window-sills. Emulsion and rubber-base paints are also suitable for woodwork. All these coatings can be used to refinish woods that have previously been painted, varnished, or shellacked. Before refinishing, make sure that all traces of wax have been removed and that any still glossy surface has been sanded so that the new coating can adhere firmly. Where there is to be a radical change of color, more than one coat may be required. If enamel or semigloss is to be used, an enamel undercoat should be applied first. Where a transparent coating is desired so that the grain of the wood will be visible, shellac or interior varnish, followed by wax, is usually favored. Open-grain woods require a filler. Stains can be used to add color to the wood.

When an opaque finish is desired for wood paneling, use the same treatment as for woodwork. You have the choice of flat, semigloss, emulsion, or rubber-base paints. When a transparent coating is desired, a wood filler should first be applied, if it is an open-grain wood. Over this, shellac or varnish, then wax, can be used. If it seems desirable to tone the wood without concealing its grain, apply a stain after the wood is filled. Over the stain, the varnish or shellac is added, followed by wax.

In basements and recreation rooms of many homes—and in many a living room, too—there are walls of brick, stone, or cinder block. Where it is desirable to coat these masonry surfaces to obstruct the invasion of moisture or to change their appearance, there are many products to choose from. Both old and new masonry walls may require a sealer or undercoat if they have not been painted before. Although you can use aluminum and casein paints on old masonry surfaces, it is not advisable to use them when the construction is brand-new. These coatings can be used on both new and old masonry, regardless of its age: enamel, semigloss, flat, cement-base, emulsion, rubber-base paint.

Wood floors can be coated with a floor paint or enamel, or they can be given a transparent finish with the aid of shellac, varnish, polyurethane, or one of the various types of stains produced for the purpose. All three types of wax (emulsion, liquid, paste) are suitable.

On stair treads, floor paint or enamel can be used, as well as floor varnish, stain, or shellac. Wax is inadvisable. On stair risers, which do not have to take the same wear and tear as treads, other types of paint that are suitable for woodwork can be used.

When steel windows are to be painted, they should first be coated with one of the metal primers especially devised for the purpose. Aluminum windows usually need no primer. Both types can be coated with aluminum or rubber-base paint, enamel, semigloss, or flat paint.

Heating ducts, radiators, and heating pipes also require a metal primer. On them, the same types of coatings can be used that are suitable for steel windows.

Steel cabinets call for a metal primer, too. Rubber-base paint, enamel, semigloss, or flat paint can be applied over it.

HOW MUCH PAINT?

Estimating your paint needs is a matter of simple arithmetic. Finish coats of good-quality paint normally cover about 500 square feet per gallon if the surface is in reasonably good condition. Primers usually cover about 450 square feet per gallon. For specific coverage rates, refer to the label on the paint you are purchasing.

On the outside of your home, you must also consider the kind of surface to be painted and its condition. Some soak up paint like blotters, whereas others provide excellent bases. For example, shingles fall far below the 500-square-feet-per-gallon rule, but clapboard is more receptive to paint. The following chart shows the approximate covering ability of house paint on various surfaces.

Surface	Square feet per gallon (approx.)	
	First Coat	Second Coat
Clapboard siding	500	550
Shingle siding	150	250
Asbestos shingles	180	400
Stucco	150	360
Cement block	180	240
Brick	200	400

1. Measure perimeter: 24′ + 40′ + 24′ + 40′ = 128′ (A)
2. Measure foundation to eave: 10′; add 2′ = 12′ (B)
3. Multiply A times B: 128′ × 12′ = 1,536 square feet
4. Measure picture window: 7′ × 10′ = 70 square feet (C)
5. Deduct 4 from 3:   1,536 sq. ft.
   − 70 sq. ft.
   1,466 sq. ft.
6. Measure roof rise = 4′ (D)
7. Measure roof run = 12′ (E)
8. Multiply D times E: 4′ × 12′ = 48′ per gable × 2 gable ends = 96 sq.ft. Add this to the square footage of the house: 1,466 + 96 = 1,562 sq.ft.
9. 1,562 sq.ft. ÷ 550 (the approximate coverage per gallon of clapboard siding for final coat) = approximately 3 gallons of paint for the house.

To determine paint requirements for your home's exterior, measure the perimeter of the home. Multiply this figure by the average height from foundation to eaves, plus two feet to allow for eaves, overhangs, and the like. Do not figure in the gable ends at this point, and make no allowances for windows and doors unless they exceed 50 square feet, as in the case of a large picture window, where you can subtract that square footage.

To figure square footage on the gable end of your house, measure the roof rise (vertical distance from eave to ridge) and the run (horizontal distance covered from eave to ridge). If the roof pitch (rise divided by run) is the same on both sides (or front and back) of the house, multiply rise by run to find the square footage needed to determine paint needs for the entire gable end. If the pitch is different on one side than on the other—as in the case of a house with a full shed dormer—figure rise and run separately for each side, multiply the figures for each side, and divide by two. Other unusually shaped protrusions, such as partial shed dormers, can be figured similarly—and will

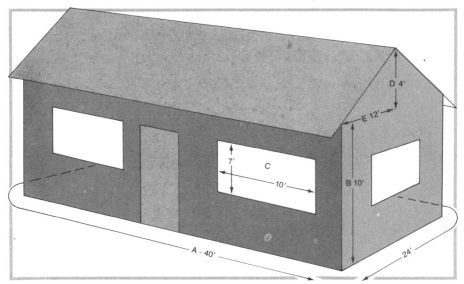

How to measure the exterior of a small house to determine paint needs.

Measuring an unequal gable end of a small house to determine the paint needs:

1. Measure the roof run: 12' (A)
2. Measure the roof rise: 10' (B)
3. Multiply A times B: 10 × 12 = 120 sq.ft. As your gable is a triangle, not a rectangle, divide by 2 = 60 sq.ft.
4. As the pitch in the drawing is different on one side than on the other, measure the other side:
   Measure the run: 14' (C), multiply by the rise 8 ' (D) = 112 sq.ft.
5. Figure out the triangle above the rectangle you just measured: the run is 14' (E); the pitch is 2' (F). Multiply E by F and divide by 2: 14 × 2 = 28 ÷ 2 = 14 sq.ft.
6. Add 3, 4, 5: 60 + 112 + 14 = 186 sq.ft. for area of gable end.

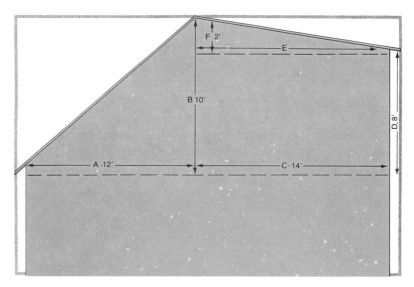

Total Area—Four Walls and Ceiling

In Square Feet

For Rooms with Ceilings 7 Feet 6 Inches High

	3'	4'	5'	6'	7'	8'	9'	10'	11'	12'	13'	14'	15'	16'	17'	18'	19'	20'	21'	22'
3'	99	117	135	153	171	189	207	225	243	261	279	297	315	333	351	369	387	405	423	441
4'	117	136	155	174	193	212	231	250	269	288	307	326	345	364	383	402	421	440	459	478
5'	135	155	175	195	215	235	255	275	295	315	335	355	375	395	415	435	455	475	495	515
6'	153	174	195	216	237	258	279	300	321	342	363	384	405	426	447	468	489	510	531	552
7'	171	193	215	237	259	281	303	325	347	369	391	413	435	457	479	501	523	545	567	589
8'	189	212	235	258	281	304	327	350	373	396	419	442	465	488	511	534	557	580	603	626
9'	207	231	255	279	303	327	351	375	399	423	447	471	495	519	543	567	591	615	639	663
10'	225	250	275	300	325	350	375	400	425	450	475	500	525	550	575	600	625	650	675	700
11'	243	269	295	321	347	373	399	425	451	477	503	529	555	581	607	633	659	685	711	737
12'	261	288	315	342	369	396	423	450	477	504	531	558	585	612	639	666	693	720	747	774
13'	279	307	335	363	391	419	447	475	503	531	559	587	615	643	671	699	727	755	783	811
14'	297	326	355	384	413	442	471	500	529	558	587	616	645	674	703	732	761	790	819	848
15'	315	345	375	405	435	465	495	525	555	585	615	645	675	705	735	765	795	825	855	885
16'	333	364	395	426	457	488	519	550	581	612	643	674	705	736	767	798	829	860	891	922
17'	351	383	415	447	479	511	543	575	607	639	671	703	735	767	799	831	863	895	927	959
18'	369	402	435	468	501	534	567	600	633	666	699	732	765	798	831	864	897	930	963	996
19'	387	421	455	489	523	557	591	625	659	693	727	761	795	829	863	897	931	965	999	1033
20'	405	440	475	510	545	580	615	650	685	720	755	790	825	860	895	930	965	1000	1035	1070
21'	423	459	495	531	567	603	639	675	711	747	783	819	855	891	927	963	999	1035	1071	1107
22'	441	478	515	552	589	626	663	700	737	774	811	848	885	922	959	996	1033	1070	1107	1144
23'	459	497	535	573	611	649	687	725	763	801	839	877	915	953	991	1029	1067	1105	1143	1181
24'	477	516	555	594	633	672	711	750	789	828	867	906	945	984	1023	1062	1101	1140	1179	1218

(*Note:* Deduct for doors, windows, archways, etc., over 50 square feet)

Total Area — Four Walls and Ceiling

In Square Feet

For Rooms with Ceilings 8 Feet High

	3'	4'	5'	6'	7'	8'	9'	10'	11'	12'	13'	14'	15'	16'	17'	18'	19'	20'	21'	22'
3'	105	124	143	162	181	200	219	238	257	276	295	314	333	352	371	390	409	428	447	466
4'	124	144	164	184	204	224	244	264	284	304	324	344	364	384	404	424	444	464	484	504
5'	143	164	185	206	227	248	269	290	311	332	353	374	395	416	437	458	479	500	521	542
6'	162	184	206	228	250	272	294	316	338	360	382	404	426	448	470	492	514	536	558	580
7'	181	204	227	250	273	296	319	342	365	388	411	434	457	480	503	526	549	572	595	618
8'	200	224	248	272	296	320	344	368	392	416	440	464	488	512	536	560	584	608	632	656
9'	219	244	269	294	319	344	369	394	419	444	469	494	519	544	569	594	619	644	669	694
10'	238	264	290	316	342	368	394	420	446	472	498	524	550	576	602	628	664	680	706	732
11'	257	284	311	338	365	392	419	446	473	500	527	554	581	608	635	662	689	716	743	770
12'	276	304	332	360	388	416	444	472	500	528	556	584	612	640	668	696	724	752	780	808
13'	295	324	353	382	411	440	469	498	527	556	585	614	643	672	701	730	759	788	817	846
14'	314	344	374	404	434	464	494	524	554	584	614	644	674	704	734	764	794	824	854	884
15'	333	364	395	426	457	488	519	550	581	612	643	674	705	736	767	798	829	860	891	922
16'	352	384	416	448	480	512	544	576	608	640	672	704	736	768	800	832	864	896	928	960
17'	371	404	437	470	503	536	569	602	635	668	701	734	767	800	833	866	899	932	965	998
18'	390	424	458	492	526	560	594	628	662	696	730	764	798	832	866	900	934	968	1002	1036
19'	409	444	479	514	549	584	619	654	689	724	759	794	829	864	899	934	969	1004	1039	1074
20'	428	464	500	536	572	608	644	680	716	752	788	824	860	896	932	968	1004	1040	1076	1112
21'	447	484	521	558	595	632	669	706	743	780	817	854	891	928	965	1002	1039	1076	1113	1150
22'	466	504	542	580	618	656	694	732	770	808	846	884	922	960	998	1036	1074	1112	1150	1188
23'	485	524	563	602	641	680	719	758	797	836	875	914	953	992	1031	1070	1109	1148	1187	1226
24'	504	544	584	624	664	704	744	784	824	864	904	944	984	1024	1064	1104	1144	1184	1224	1264

(*Note:* Deduct for doors, windows, archways, etc., over 50 square feet)

Total Area Four Walls and Ceiling

In Square Feet

For Rooms with Ceilings 9 Feet High

	3'	4'	5'	6'	7'	8'	9	10'	11'	12'	13'	14'	15'	16'	17'	18'	19'	20'	21'	22'
3'	117	138	159	180	201	222	243	264	285	306	327	348	369	390	411	432	453	474	495	516
4'	138	160	182	204	226	248	270	292	314	336	358	380	402	424	446	468	490	512	534	556
5'	159	182	205	228	251	274	297	320	343	366	389	412	435	458	481	504	527	550	573	596
6'	180	204	228	252	276	300	324	348	372	396	420	444	468	492	516	540	564	588	612	636
7'	201	226	251	276	301	326	351	376	401	426	451	476	501	526	551	576	601	626	651	676
8'	222	248	274	300	326	352	378	404	430	456	482	508	534	560	586	612	638	664	690	716
9'	243	270	297	324	351	378	405	432	459	486	513	540	567	594	621	648	675	702	729	756
10'	264	292	320	348	376	404	432	460	488	516	544	572	600	628	656	684	712	740	768	796
11'	285	314	343	372	401	430	459	488	517	546	575	604	633	662	691	720	749	778	807	836
12'	306	336	366	396	426	456	486	516	546	576	606	636	666	696	726	756	786	816	846	876
13'	327	358	389	420	451	482	513	544	575	606	637	668	699	730	761	792	823	854	885	916
14'	348	380	412	444	476	508	540	572	604	636	668	700	732	764	796	828	860	892	924	956
15'	369	402	435	468	501	534	567	600	633	666	699	732	765	798	831	864	897	930	963	996
16'	390	424	458	492	526	560	594	628	662	696	730	764	798	832	866	900	934	968	1002	1036
17'	411	446	481	516	551	586	621	656	691	726	761	796	831	866	901	936	971	1006	1041	1076
18'	432	468	504	540	576	612	648	684	720	756	792	828	864	900	936	972	1008	1044	1080	1116
19'	453	490	527	564	601	638	675	712	749	786	823	860	897	934	971	1008	1045	1082	1119	1156
20'	474	512	550	588	626	664	702	740	778	816	854	892	930	968	1006	1044	1082	1120	1158	1196
21'	495	534	573	612	651	690	729	768	807	846	885	924	963	1002	1041	1080	1119	1158	1197	1236
22'	516	556	596	636	676	716	756	796	836	876	916	956	996	1036	1076	1116	1156	1196	1236	1276
23'	537	578	619	660	701	742	783	824	865	906	947	988	1029	1070	1111	1152	1193	1234	1275	1316
24'	558	600	612	684	726	768	810	852	894	936	978	1020	1062	1104	1146	1188	1230	1272	1314	1356

(*Note:* Deduct for doors, windows, archways, etc., over 50 square feet)

Total Area—Four Walls and Ceiling

In Square Feet

For Rooms with Ceilings 10 Feet High

	3'	4'	5'	6'	7'	8'	9'	10'	11'	12'	13'	14'	15'	16'	17'	18'	19'	20'	21'	22'
3'	129	152	175	198	221	244	267	290	313	336	359	382	405	428	451	474	497	520	543	566
4'	152	176	200	224	248	272	296	320	344	368	392	416	440	464	488	512	536	560	584	608
5'	175	200	225	250	275	300	325	350	375	400	425	450	475	500	525	550	575	600	625	650
6'	198	224	250	276	302	328	354	380	406	432	458	484	510	536	562	588	614	640	666	692
7'	221	248	275	302	329	356	383	410	437	464	491	518	545	572	599	626	653	680	707	734
8'	244	272	300	328	356	384	412	440	468	496	524	552	580	608	636	664	692	720	748	776
9'	267	296	325	354	383	412	441	479	499	528	557	586	615	644	673	702	731	760	789	818
10'	290	320	350	380	410	440	470	500	530	560	590	620	650	680	710	740	770	800	830	860
11'	313	344	375	406	437	468	499	530	561	592	623	654	685	716	747	778	809	840	871	902
12'	336	368	400	432	464	496	528	560	592	624	656	688	720	752	784	816	848	880	912	944
13'	359	392	425	458	491	524	557	590	623	656	689	722	755	788	821	854	887	920	953	986
14'	382	416	450	484	518	552	586	620	654	688	722	756	790	824	858	892	926	960	994	1028
15'	405	440	475	510	545	580	615	650	685	720	755	790	825	860	895	930	965	1000	1035	1070
16'	428	464	500	536	572	608	644	680	716	752	788	824	860	896	932	968	1004	1040	1076	1112
17'	451	488	525	562	599	636	673	710	747	784	821	858	895	932	969	1006	1043	1080	1117	1154
18'	474	512	550	588	626	664	702	740	778	816	854	892	930	968	1006	1044	1082	1120	1158	1196
19'	497	536	575	614	653	692	731	770	809	848	887	926	965	1004	1043	1082	1121	1160	1199	1238
20'	520	560	600	640	680	720	760	800	840	880	920	960	1000	1040	1080	1120	1160	1200	1240	1280
21'	543	584	625	666	707	748	789	830	871	912	953	994	1035	1076	1117	1158	1199	1240	1281	1322
22'	566	608	650	692	734	776	818	860	902	944	986	1028	1070	1112	1154	1196	1238	1280	1322	1364
23'	589	632	675	718	761	804	847	890	933	976	1019	1062	1105	1148	1191	1234	1277	1320	1363	1406
24'	612	656	700	744	788	832	876	920	964	1008	1052	1096	1140	1184	1228	1272	1316	1360	1404	1448

(*Note:* Deduct for doors, windows, archways, etc., over 50 square feet)

put to use the knowledge you acquired in those seemingly fruitless hours you spent in high-school geometry class. There was a reason, after all!

Estimating interior paint needs is done in the same way, by determining square footage of walls and ceilings, then dividing the total by the coverage shown on the paint-can label. Again, do not allow for a window or door opening unless it exceeds 50 square feet. The tables show total area for four walls and ceiling of rooms at the most common heights. If the ceiling is to be painted a different color, figure it separately and de-duct the square footage from the figure given in the appropriate table.

It's always a good idea to buy an extra gallon or quart of paint to make sure that you have enough on hand when you set about doing the job—especially if you are a weekend painter. It is extremely frustrating to run out of paint with just a few more feet of wall to go; and when this happens on a Saturday evening right after the paint store has closed, the frustration is dragged out interminably. Better sufficient than sorry, and almost all paint dealers will take back unopened cans of paint.

3
Painting Tools

THE WORLD IS full of painting experts. Because painting is a relatively easy do-it-yourself task, and because many amateurs become "professionals" merely by hanging out a shingle and advertising in the classified ad sections of the local newspaper, there is a great deal of dogmatic, if misinformed, rhetoric about proper painting methods—especially the brush vs. roller vs. spray controversy.

There are still many old-timers who disdain the roller, and as for the spray gun—well, its use should be limited by law to applying pesticides to rose bushes, and never paint to a house! For these purists, only a brush can truly communicate with a surface being coated, "working in" the paint for a properly applied finish.

On the other hand, there are those who recoil in horror at the thought of picking up paint with anything other than a roller, which they regard as the greatest invention since (and an extension of) the wheel. And there are those adherents of spray painting who regard the wielders of both brush and roller as throwbacks to the age when man's use of paint was limited to decorating the walls of his cave with crude drawings of animals.

The fact is that all three methods of applying paint have distinct advantages (and disadvantages). If there is any hard-and-fast rule to follow when it comes to selecting and using these tools, it is: Use what works best for you.

COMPARISON CHART: BRUSH vs. ROLLER vs. SPRAYER

	Small Brush	Wide Brush	Roller	Sprayer
ADVANTAGES	Maneuverability Low price Easy to use Easy to clean	Quick application Versatile Smooth finish Can cut in around trim	Speed over large sur- faces Easy to use Low price	Fast, easy to use Smoothest finish Has other uses
DISADVANTAGES	Takes more time on large jobs	Requires some experi- ence for best results	Must cut in with brush or corner roller Difficult to clean covers	Difficult to use indoors Difficult to cut in fine line Requires some experi- ence for good results Not worthwhile for small jobs
TYPE JOBS BEST SUITED FOR	Trim, sash Cabinetwork Radiators, blinds, etc.	Walls, exteriors, large surfaces	Large unbroken sur- faces Rough surfaces (stuc- co, block, etc.) Floors	Large exterior surfaces "Hard to paint" surfaces (wicker, stucco, blinds)
RELATIVE COST	39¢ to $5.00	99¢ to $15.00	$1.99 to $7.50	$9.95 to $1000.00 (commercial type)

PAINTBRUSHES

Quality is a very important factor in selecting a brush, regardless of the size or style needed for a particular project. A good brush will hold more paint and enable you to apply the paint more smoothly and with less effort.

All good brushes have bristles that are "flagged," a term denoting splits on the bristle end. The more "flags" the better, as they help retain paint. Hog bristle is naturally flagged; synthetic bristle is artificially flagged, or split.

Test for "bounce" by brushing bristles against the back of your hand. In a good brush, the bristles will feel elastic and springy. When the brush is gently pressed on any surface, the bristles will not fan out excessively.

Check the setting. Bristles should be solidly set to prevent any chance of fallout during painting. Jar the brush and fan the bristles. Any loose bristles will be apparent. The metal band holding the bristles is called a ferrule. Stainless steel and aluminum are generally used on better-grade brushes for greater resistance to corrosion.

Both the surface area and type of paint determine the size and style of brush to be used. Calcimine brushes with very long, tough, and elastic gray hog bristles are best for applying water-thinned paints to large areas. Enamel and varnish brushes, both flat and chisel-shaped, are best for applying oil-base paints and lacquers. The shape and length of the latter type help secure a smoother flow and prevent lap marks.

The following brush styles and sizes are recommended for most painting projects around the home:

• Flat wall brushes: Sizes vary from 3 to 6 inches in width with thicknesses of ¾ to 1½ inches and bristles from 2 to 7 inches long. They are best suited for painting large surfaces such as walls, ceilings, and floors.

Flagged bristles.

Wall brushes.

Pressing the brush on a surface to test for "bounce."

Fan brush to check loose bristles.

Flat, chisel-shaped varnish brushes.

Sash, trim, artist's brushes.

• Varnish brushes: Sizes range from 1 to 3½ inches in width, with bristles from 2 to 4½ inches long. They are ideally suited for painting baseboards, window frames, narrow boards, or enameling and varnishing furniture and small panels.

• Round sash and flat trim brushes: Sizes range from 1 to 1½ inches in width. Trellises, screens, small pipes, toys, and all

Fishtailing of brush caused by
not using it properly.

Standing the brush on its tip
causes the edges to bend.

Cleaning brush in thinner.

Washing brush.

Wrapping brush in paper.

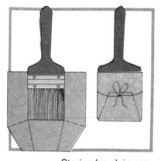

Storing brush in can.

Before reuse of brush,
recondition it.

Priming the brush.

small areas are best painted with sash, trim, or even small artist's brushes.

In addition to these general styles, most dealers carry special brushes for bronzing, roofing, stippling, and stenciling.

A quality brush is a fine tool and should be properly used and cared for. For example, a wide brush should never be used to paint pipes and similar surfaces. This causes the brush to "fishtail." A brush should never be left standing on its bristles. The weight causes the edge to bend and curl, ruining the fine painting tips.

Always clean a brush while it is still soft after painting. Use the thinner for the product in which the brush has been used. For example, turpentine followed by naphtha or mineral spirits should be used to remove oil-base paints in which turpentine is a recommended thinning ingredient. Alcohol or lacquer thinner are used on brushes after applying shellac or alcohol-base stains. Cleaning should be followed by washing the brush in soap and water. Latex or water-base paints can be easily removed by dissolving the excess paint in water.

Once the brush is thoroughly cleaned, it should be properly stored. Drill a hole in the brush handle, insert a wire rod through the hole, then rest the rod on a paint, coffee, or shortening can taller than the length of the bristles. Bristles should not rest on the bottom of the can.

For long-term storage, make sure that the bristles are completely dry, then wrap the brush in foil or heavy paper. Hang by the handle in an out-of-the-way place.

Before reusing the brush, work it back and forth across your fingers or palm of the hand to remove dust, dirt, or loose bristling material. If the brush is to be used in shellac, water-base, or latex paint, it should be washed in soap and water and thoroughly dried before painting.

For best results prime the brush by dipping into the paint halfway to the ferrule.

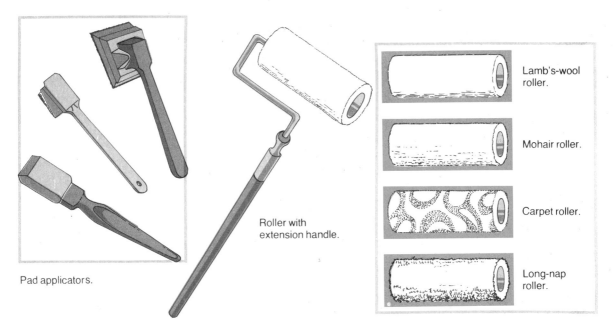

Pad applicators.

Roller with
extension handle.

Lamb's-wool
roller.

Mohair roller.

Carpet roller.

Long-nap
roller.

Then tap lightly, five or six times, against the top edge of your paint container. The brush is now ready to use.

PAD APPLICATORS

Relatively new are pad applicators. These are similar to brushes but generally cheaper (except for throwaway brushes). On smooth surfaces, they also apply paint much faster than brushes. Made of foamed urethane for use on both interior and exterior surfaces, some of them have replaceable pads. Others are cheap enough that it is more practical to discard them after use rather than attempt to clean them.

PAINT ROLLERS

Painting with a roller is probably the easiest and quickest method for the average do-it-yourself decorator. It is important to use a roller that is suitable for the kind of paint to be applied. Lambs'-wool rollers, for ex-

ample, are excellent with oil-base paints, but they should not be used with enamels or water-thinned latex paints because these paints will cause the wool to mat, rendering the roller unusable.

Mohair rollers can be used with any type of interior flat paint, but they are especially recommended for applying enamel and for use when a smooth finish is desired. Rollers made from synthetic fibers can also be used with all types of flat paint, inside and out. If a stipple finish is desired, use a roller made of carpeting.

Another factor to consider is the length of the nap or pile, which can range from 1/16 to 1½ inches. A handy rule to remember is: the smoother the surface, the shorter the nap; the rougher the surface, the longer the nap. Use short-napped rollers for most walls, ceilings, woodwork, and smooth concrete. The longer naps are for masonry, brick, and other irregular surfaces.

For walls and ceilings the best size roller for the amateur is the 7- or 9-inch model. (Extension handles make it possible to paint ceilings without a ladder.) For finish-

Trim roller.

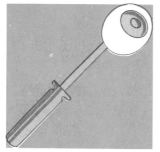

Cutting-in roller.

Corner roller.

Edging roller.

most vacuum cleaners, to large pressure-feed air compressors available for a low rental fee in most areas. Suction-feed spray equipment is satisfactory . for most household projects. Before deciding to spray paint, however, you should consider whether the time saved will be consumed in the extra work of masking windows and other areas not to be painted.

Although practically any paint product that can be brushed or rolled on can be applied with spray equipment, spray painting is best suited for covering large wall areas, fences, or furniture items that can be painted in an open space.

The width of the spray fan should be ad-

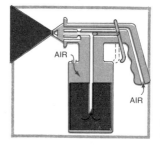

Suction-feed sprayer.

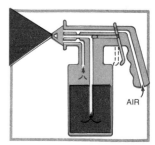

Pressure-feed sprayer.

ing woodwork, doors, and trim, the best choice is the 3-inch model. Smaller sizes are available for cutting in corners and for use on window frames and moldings. There are even V-edged rollers that coat both sides of a corner at the same time. To help you paint a wall without getting the paint on the ceiling there are special edging rollers.

Before applying paint with a roller, first cut in the edges of the wall with a brush or with an edging roller, taking care not to get paint on the ceiling or adjacent wall.

PAINT SPRAYERS

Since the invention of the spray gun for mass-production industrial painting, it has become increasingly popular as a practical and economical means of applying paint by professional and amateur alike.

Sizes range from the small suction-feed spray-painting attachments available with

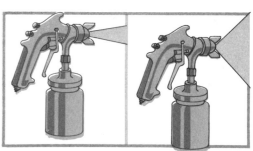

Adjust width of fan to size of article to be coated.

justed to the size of the article being coated. A narrow fan is best for spraying small or narrow articles; a full-width fan should be used to spray walls.

Prepainting practice is important. The handyman should test the thickness of the paint, the size of the fan, and the motion of the spray gun before painting any surface. Excessive thickness can cause rippling of the wet film by the spraying air or lead to blistering later. On vertical and inclined surfaces, it can cause running or sagging.

The spray fan should be pointed perpendicularly to the surface being coated. The stroke or motion of the hand holding the spray gun should be started while the spray is pointed beyond the surface to be painted. This assures a smooth, even flow when you reach the surface itself.

Move the gun parallel to the surface, aiming beyond the edge of the surface and moving with an even stroke back and forth across the area. Corners and edges should be sprayed first.

Although a pressure-feed gun will handle heavier paint, the compressor unit poses a safety problem. Motors or gas engines of air-compressing outfits should be operated outside the spray area to avoid hazards from explosion and fire. The unit should also be placed in an area where it will receive a continuous supply of fresh, clean, dry air. Dust or vapor entering the air intake will decrease the efficiency of the unit and affect the results.

Regardless of the type of equipment used, every precaution should be taken by the spray operator. Skin should be protected. The area being sprayed should be well ventilated. A fire extinguisher should be available for use if needed, and all flammable liquids should be kept in safety cans.

Spray equipment should be thoroughly cleaned immediately after use. Simple cleaning can be done by spraying a suitable solvent through the equipment. A broom

Hold sprayer perpendicular to the surface to be coated.

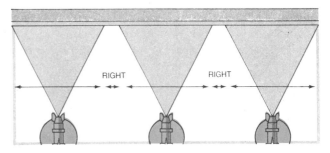

Move sprayer parallel to surface.

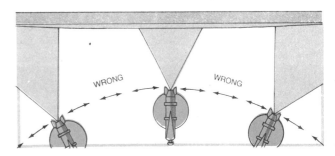

Cleaning fluid tip with broom straw.

straw can be used to unclog the fluid tip. Never use a metal wire or nail to clear air holes in the spray tip; the precision-machined openings are easily damaged.

Hook scraper.   Wall scraper.

Putty knife.   Razor-blade scraper.

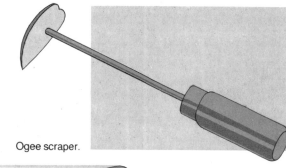

Ogee scraper.

Wire brush with handle.

Wire brush without handle.

OTHER TOOLS OF THE PAINTER'S TRADE

A variety of scrapers should be in every amateur (and professional, for that matter) painter's tool kit. Hook scrapers are good for rough exterior surfaces, and are often used with paint remover. Wall scrapers are handy for removing old paint and general scraping and cleaning. They come in various widths up to 5 inches; a 3- or 4-inch size with a stiff blade will meet most of your needs. A putty knife, similar in appearance to a narrow wall scraper, can also be used for scraping and cleaning, as well as applying and smoothing putty. An "ogee" scraper is the tool for removing old paint from crevices and recesses that can't be reached by flat scrapers. A razor-blade scraper is best for scraping paint off glass if your cutting-in is not quite perfect (and whose is?).

Wire brushes are handy for removing grime and surface dirt before applying exterior paint. Sandpaper is another important tool for smoothing surfaces. It is best used with a sanding block. When heavy sanding is required, a power belt sander may be used, followed by a finishing sander for final smoothing.

A propane torch is sometimes used to soften old paint for scraping, but this procedure entails certain obvious risks. An electric paint softener accomplishes the same end much more safely.

A calking gun is needed to seal cracks around doors, windows, corners, and other areas before exterior painting. In addition, an assortment of common tools will be helpful: hammer and nailset for driving in nails that may have come loose, a chisel for prying molding away from walls, a screwdriver for removing switch and receptacle covers, hinges, and other hardware.

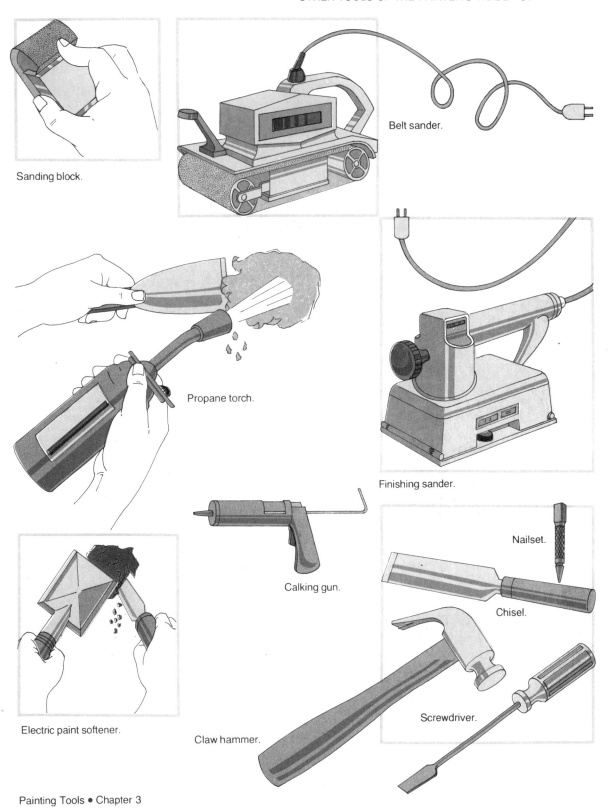

Sanding block.

Belt sander.

Propane torch.

Finishing sander.

Calking gun.

Nailset.

Chisel.

Screwdriver.

Electric paint softener.

Claw hammer.

Painting Tools • Chapter 3

4

Ladders

OF ALL THE "tools" you need for painting, perhaps none is more important than a ladder, because it involves your personal safety. Unless you limit your paint job to the base woodwork, or are built with the reach of a pro basketball center, you will have to get "up there," whether to do the ceiling or the upper reaches of your home's exterior. Accept no substitutes for a ladder—standing on a chair is risky business and makes the job a lot more tedious, too. The range of ladder designs, types, sizes, and materials is broad enough to fit any need.

Before you make a trip to the store to buy a ladder, think about your needs. Will the ladder be used indoors or outdoors? How high will you want to climb? Who will be using it? Where will it be stored?

If you live in an apartment, a stepladder will probably meet all your needs and will be easy to handle. Its size will depend on the highest point you want to reach, bearing in mind that you should not stand higher than the step below the ladder top. Never stand on the top of a stepladder!

If you live in a house, you may need two ladders—a stepladder for indoor work and a straight ladder or extension ladder for use outdoors. The outdoor ladder should be long enough to extend a minimum of 3 feet higher than the highest area you want to reach.

SHOPPING FOR A LADDER

Don't let price alone guide you. Select a ladder according to your needs. And don't let the salesperson hurry you into making a quick purchase. Check the ladder for weak steps, loose rungs, or other weaknesses before you take it from the store.

Don't buy an unidentified ladder. Be sure that the name of the manufacturer or distributor is on the label. This information may be important in case of a quality problem or an accident.

Look for a seal affixed to the ladder indicating that it conforms to the standards of the American National Standards Institute (ANSI) or the Underwriters' Laboratories, Inc. (UL). The absence of a seal, however, does not necessarily imply that the ladder is of poor quality.

MATERIALS

Wood, aluminum, magnesium, and fiberglass are the principal materials used in the construction of ladders. Each type has its advantages and disadvantages.

Wood ladders are sturdy and bend little under loads for which they are designed. They are heavier than metal ladders, and large sizes are harder to handle. When dry, wood ladders are safe to use around electrical circuits or when you are working with power tools.

If wood ladders are used indoors, or adequately protected from moisture and sunlight when used outdoors, they will last a long time. Unprotected in the open, however, they may be attacked by wood-destroying insects, weakened by rot, or cracked and split by the action of sun and rain. Once weakened, wood may break easily and suddenly.

Metal ladders are generally a little more expensive than wood ladders of the same quality, but they last longer because they do not deteriorate from moisture and sunlight and are not susceptible to attack by insects. Aluminum and magnesium ladders are comparatively light, weighing only about two-thirds as much as those made of wood. The two metals weigh about the same, but magnesium ladders are somewhat more expensive. (Magnesium is actually a lighter metal than aluminum but not as strong; therefore, side rails and legs are constructed with thicker cross sections to provide comparable strength.) Magnesium corrodes (turns black) more than aluminum and has less impact resistance. Aluminum and magnesium ladders are not recommended for use around electrical circuits.

Fiberglass is the newest ladder material to appear on the market. It is used to make the side rails of high-grade metal stepladders and of straight and extension ladders. The result is a nonconductive ladder that is

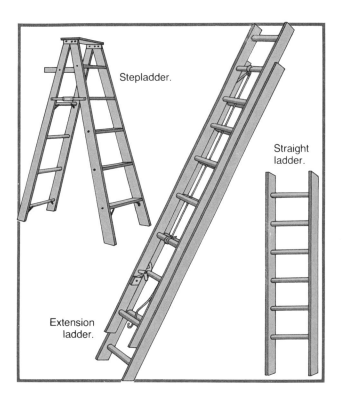

Stepladder.

Straight ladder.

Extension ladder.

light, corrosion-resistant, serviceable, and practically maintenance-free. These ladders do not dry-rot or absorb moisture, and the fiberglass side rails have greater impact resistance than wood, aluminum, or magnesium. These ladders, however, are quite expensive and are used mostly by professionals.

LADDER CODES

The stepladder and the extension ladder are the two types most commonly used around the home. Codes have been established by the American National Standards Institute to cover wood and metal stepladders and extension ladders. Any ladder you buy with an ANSI seal conforms to the code.

The code for wood ladders is a dimensional one. It covers, for example, the

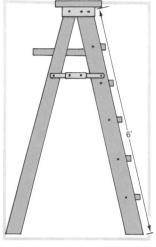

Stepladder size.

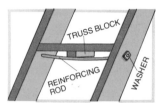

Wood stepladder metal angle brace.

Wood stepladder reinforcing rod.

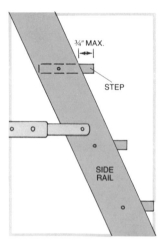

Maximum protrusion of wood steps beyond rails.

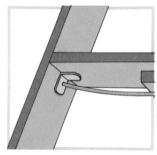

Fastening wood steps with metal angles.

Fastening wood steps in grooves.

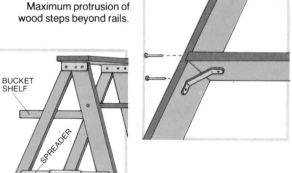

Spreader and bucket shelf.

depth and thickness of steps. Performance tests have not been developed. The code for metal ladders is based on performance. It prescribes the methods for testing the strength of ladders, with emphasis on side rails, steps, fastening hardware, and the back legs of stepladders.

STEPLADDERS

A stepladder is a self-supporting portable ladder. It is nonadjustable in length, and it has flat steps and a hinged back. Size is determined by the length of the ladder measured along the front edge of the side rails. Stepladders are useful for many indoor and outdoor jobs where the height to be reached is low and the ladder can be rested on a firm surface.

Both wood and metal stepladders are available in three categories. They are: Type I, heavy duty (250 pounds load-carrying capacity); Type II, medium duty (225 pounds); and Type III, light duty (200 pounds). These categories are accepted and widely used by the ladder industry. Look for duty rating when you purchase your new stepladder.

Steps on a wooden stepladder should be flat, parallel, and level when the ladder is open. There should not be more than 12 inches between steps, and these should be at least ¾ inch thick and at least 3½ inches deep (1 x 4 nominal size).

Each step should be braced either with metal angle braces or a metal reinforcing rod. Ends of reinforcing rods should pass through metal washers of sufficient thickness to prevent pressing into and damaging the side rails. When metal reinforcing rods are used, a wood or metal truss block should be fitted to the bottom of each step and positioned at the center between the rod and the step. The bottom step should be reinforced with metal angle braces securely attached to the step and to each side rail. Steps should not protrude more than ¾ inch beyond the front of the side rail and should have no splits, cracks, chips, knots, or other imperfections.

Steps should be fastened to the side rails with metal brackets or by grooving. At least two 6d nails (or equivalent) should be used at each end of the step, through the side rail into the step.

The metal spreader or locking device should be large and strong enough to hold the front and back sections securely in the open position. It should be resistant to rust and corrosion. The bucket shelf should be capable of holding 25 pounds and should fold completely within the ladder. Feet should be level in open position. They can be equipped with safety shoes to prevent slippage or lateral movement.

The slope in the open position should be a minimum of 3½ inches per foot of length of the front section and a minimum of 2 inches per foot of length of the back section. The width between the side rails at the top step should be no less than 12 inches and should increase toward the bottom of the ladder at a minimum rate of 1 inch per foot of length.

Metal stepladder steps should be flat, parallel, and level when the ladder is open. Steps should be corrugated, have raised patterns, be dimpled, be coated with skid-resistant materials, or otherwise treated to minimize the possibility of slipping. There should be no more than 12 inches between steps, as with wood ladders.

The depth of the step or tread should be not less than 3 inches for 225- or 250-pound capacity ladders, or 2½ inches for 200-pound capacity. Steps should have no sharp edges and should not be bent or dented. The bottom step should always be reinforced with metal angle braces.

If steps have only one fastener on each side, there should be diagonal metal braces

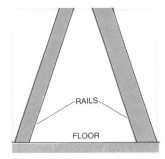

Feet should be level when ladder is open.

Safety shoes for wood stepladder.

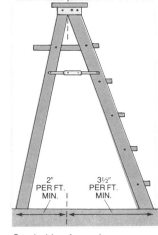

Stepladder slope when open.

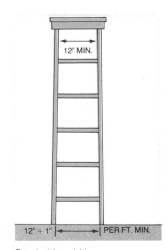

Stepladder width.

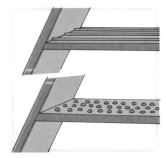

Corrugated and dimpled metal stepladder steps.

Braces on metal stepladder steps.

under both top and bottom steps. If steps have two fastenings on each side, the ladder should have diagonal metal braces under the bottom step.

Shoes on bottom of metal stepladder rails (top left).

Folded bucket shelf (top right).

Extension trestle ladder.

Trestle ladder.

Platform ladder (left).

Testing stepladder stability.

The bucket shelf should be capable of holding 50 pounds and should fold completely within the ladder. The bottoms of the four rails should be covered for safety with insulating material, such as rubber or plastic nonslip shoes. Spreader, slope, and width specifications are the same as for wood stepladders.

Before purchasing a stepladder, test its stability by climbing to the second step from the bottom and shaking the ladder moderately back and forth while you hold onto the side rails. If the ladder feels loose, consider purchasing a heavier-duty one or one made by another manufacturer.

STEPLADDER VARIATIONS

There are three other types of ladders that are closely related to the stepladder: the platform ladder, the trestle ladder, and the extension trestle ladder. While these ladders are primarily for professional use, they may also come in handy for use around the home.

One type of platform ladder has a guardrail that lessens the danger of falling. It should have widely spaced legs to provide for good balance. Two of these ladders, used in tandem, provide a good, sturdy base for a scaffold.

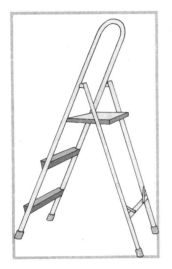

Platform ladder with guardrail.

Platform ladders used to support scaffold.

EXTENSION LADDERS

An extension ladder consists of two or more straight sections traveling in guides or brackets arranged to permit length adjustment. Its size is designated by the sum of the length of the sections, measured along the side rails.

Each section of an opened extension ladder should overlap the adjacent section by a minimum number of feet, depending on overall length. If an extension ladder is up to 36 feet in length, the overlap should be 3 feet; if total length is between 36 and 48 feet, overlap should be 4 feet. The ladder should be equipped with positive stops to ensure that it cannot be opened too far.

To eliminate confusion in identifying the length of an extension ladder because of

overlap, the Federal Trade Commission requires that the total length and working length be clearly marked. For example: "Maximum working length 17 feet; total length of sections 20 feet."

To help you choose the right size extension ladder for your needs, the accompanying table shows the recommended relation between working height for a ladder and total length of sections. The recommended total length of sections allows for the proper overlap plus 3 feet more than the greatest working height. The extra 3 feet is the minimum required for safe use.

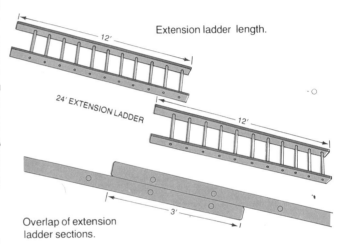

Extension ladder length.

Overlap of extension ladder sections.

Recommended Lengths for Different Heights of Extension Ladders

Height You Want to Reach	Recommended Length of Sections
9½ feet	16 feet
13½ feet	20 feet
17½ feet	24 feet
21½ feet	28 feet
24½ feet	32 feet
29 feet	36 feet
33 feet	40 feet
36½ feet	44 feet

Safety boot for wood
extension ladder.

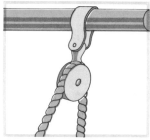

Extension ladder pulley.

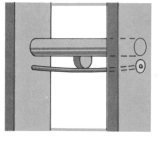

Reinforcement of bottom rung
on wood extension ladder.

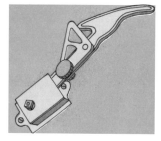

Rung lock.

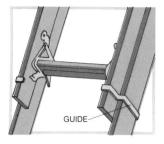

GUIDE

Side-rail slide guide.

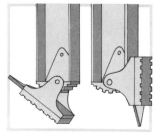

Safety shoes for metal
extension ladder.

Metal ladder rungs: round,
round with flat surface.

Flat surface horizontal when
ladder is at 75° angle.

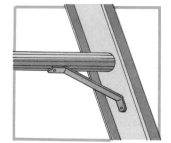

Brace for metal
bottom rung.

Feet of wooden extension ladders may be equipped with safety boots or shoes, which are sometimes offered as an accessory. Pulleys should not be less than 1¼ inches outside diameter, and ropes not less than 5/16 inch diameter, with minimum breaking strength of 500 pounds. Rungs must be round and of hard wood, free from crossgrain, splits, cracks, chips, or knots. They should be not less than 1⅛ inches in diameter and spaced not more than 12 inches apart.

Although not required by standards of ANSI or UL, it is highly desirable that at least the bottom rung be reinforced with a truss rod. Safety rung locks should be resistant to or protected against rust and corrosion. Locks may be of either the spring or gravity type. Side-rail slide guides should be securely attached and placed to prevent the upper section from tipping or falling out while the ladder is being raised or lowered.

Width of wooden ladders should be not less than 12 inches between rails of the upper section. For the lower section, width should be a minimum of 14½ inches up to and including 28-foot ladders, and 16 inches for longer ladders.

Feet of metal extension ladders should have rubber, plastic, or other slip-resistant safety treads or shoes secured to foot brackets. The brackets should pivot freely to rest squarely when the ladder is inclined for use. Rungs should be round or round with flat step surface, and with a slip-resistant tread. The flat surface should be horizontal when the ladder is placed at a 75-degree angle. The top and bottom rungs should be not more than 12 inches from the ends of the side rails to provide for extra strength and stability.

Rung braces are not required by standards of ANSI or UL, but it is highly desirable that at least the bottom rung be reinforced with a metal rung brace.

The width of metal ladders varies. The upper section should be not less than 12 inches. Bottom sections are not less than 12½ inches for ladders up to 16 feet, 14 inches for ladders up to 28 feet, and 15 inches for ladders up to 40 feet. Ropes, pulleys, and safety rung locks are the same as for wooden ladders. On most aluminum extension ladders, the side rails interlock, eliminating the need for slide guides.

LADDER ACCESSORIES

A number of useful ladder accessories can add substantially to your safety and convenience. Trays are available for attachment to extension ladders to hold paint, tools, or work materials. Safety shoes should be attached to all metal ladders and to all wood ladders used in slippery or wet places. Although metal ladders are usually sold equipped with safety shoes, wear may make replacement necessary. Shoes for wood ladders are usually bought as accessory items.

Safety wall-grips of rubber or plastic strips can be attached to the tops of extension ladder side rails. These strips keep the top of a ladder from slipping on the surface against which it leans.

MAINTENANCE

Wood ladders to be used or stored outdoors should be protected with a coat or two of clear sealer, spar varnish, shellac, or

Safety rung lock on metal extension ladder.

Interlocking side rails.

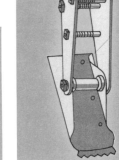

Two types of replacement safety shoes.

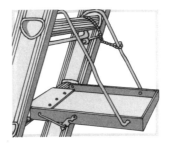

Tray for extension ladder.

Wall grips.

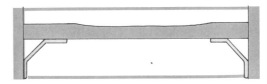

Replace worn ladder steps.

a clear wood preservative. Do not paint wood ladders since this would prevent periodic visual inspection of their condition. Linseed oil will help to rustproof metal parts such as rung locks.

Replace worn or frayed ropes on exten-

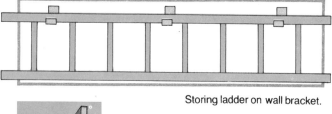

Storing ladder on wall bracket.

Wall bracket.

sion ladders. Check the condition of any ladder that has been dropped or has fallen before it is used again. Replace steps on wood stepladders when approximately one-fourth worn away.

Ladders should be stored where they will not be exposed to the elements. Wood ladders should be kept in a well-ventilated location, away from dampness and excessive heat. Store straight or extension ladders in flat racks or on wall brackets to prevent sag. If long ladders are stored horizontally, use three or more hangers for support.

LADDER SAFETY

Inspect the ladder before each use. Oil moving parts and tighten loose fasteners. Check the rope and pulley on an extension ladder for wear and breaking strength.

Set up long straight or extension ladders by the following method to avoid muscle strain or losing control of the ladder:

• Brace the lower end of the ladder against something solid so that it cannot slide.

• Grasp the uppermost rung, using both hands, then raise the top end and walk forward under the ladder, moving your hands to grasp other rungs as you proceed.

• When the ladder is erect, move it to the desired location and then lean it forward to the top resting point.

• Place ladders at the correct angle with the wall. The base of the ladder should be one-quarter of its working length away from the wall or support. If the ladder is placed at too great an angle—that is, with the base too far out—it is subject to strain that can cause it to break or slip. On the other hand, if the base of the ladder is too close to the wall, the ladder is likely to tip backward.

• Place your ladder so that it has a firm footing. The feet of either a stepladder or an extension ladder should be level. If the ground is uneven or soft under one foot, brace the ladder. If necessary, the ladder should be lashed or held in place to prevent slippage.

• Adjust the length of an extension ladder only when your eye level is below the level of the locking device so that you can see when the lock is engaged.

When using an extension or straight ladder, be sure that it is the proper length to reach the desired height. For example, in using an extension ladder to reach a roof, be sure the top of the ladder extends at least 3 feet above the roof edge. Don't climb up an extension ladder so far that you have to reach down to grasp the side rails.

Never climb higher than the step below the top of a stepladder. If you stand on the top, you can lose your balance.

Go up and down a ladder carefully, always facing the ladder. Carry your tools or other work materials in your clothing or attached to a belt. Take one step at a time.

Move the ladder to where the work can be done without reaching far to one side of the ladder. Overreaching can cause you and the ladder to fall.

Be extremely careful when using metal or wet wood ladders around electrical circuits, power tools, or appliances. Metal and wet wood conduct electricity. Always play it safe!

Brace lower end and "walk" ladder upright.

Place ladder in desired position.

Support ladder on uneven or unstable ground (above and below).

Place ladder at correct angle, neither too far away nor too close.

Don't go so high that you have to reach down to rails (left) and don't overreach (right).

5

Interior Painting

IN GENERAL, walls, ceilings, woodwork, and other surfaces to be painted should be clean, dry, and smooth. But read the label on the paint can before you start painting; it may contain additional or special instructions for preparing the surface.

PREPARING NEW PLASTER AND WALLBOARD

New plaster walls should not be painted with oil-base paint until they have been thoroughly cured—usually after about two months. Then a primer coat should be applied first.

If necessary to paint uncured plaster, apply only one coat of a latex paint or primer. Latex, or water-base, paint is not affected by the alkali in new plaster and allows water to escape while the plaster dries. Subsequent coats of paint—either oil-base or latex—can be added when the plaster is thoroughly cured.

Unpainted plaster readily picks up and absorbs dirt and is difficult to clean. The one coat of latex paint or primer will protect plaster walls.

On new wallboard or drywall, a latex primer or paint is recommended for the first coat. Solvent-thinned paints tend to cause a rough surface. After the first coat of latex paint, subsequent coats can be of either type. Clean or dust new surfaces before you apply the first coat of primer or paint.

PREPARING OLDER SURFACES

Most homes built in the past 25 to 30 years have walls and ceilings covered with wallboard, also known as gypsumboard, drywall, or plasterboard. Before painting, make minor or major repairs as necessary. Look in particular for cracks around windows and door frames, nails that have raised the surface, and just plain holes.

"Popped" nails.

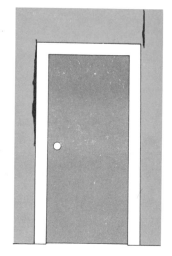

Cracks around door frames.

Drive ringed nail near popped nail.

Use a nailset to avoid damaging wallboard.

Apply spackle with a broad or putty knife.

Wood in heated homes contracts in the winter and expands in the summer, and this can cause nail "popping."

Drive popped nails back below the surface of the wallboard. Reinforce weak areas by driving a ringed drywall nail into the panel below or above a popped nail about an inch or two away. Drive the nail until it dimples the surface and no more; use a nailset to avoid banging up the wallboard and causing major damage.

Use spackle to patch the dimples and even the surface. Spackle comes in powdered or ready-mixed form. Apply it with a broad knife or putty knife, filling the area, scraping off the excess, and sanding to an even surface when dry.

Cracks can be sealed with fiberglass tape or with perforated drywall tape and joint cement. Sand the area of the crack 4 inches or so to each side when using perforated tape, then apply joint cement over the crack. Center the strip of perforated tape over the crack, pressing it flat with a broad knife. Remove excess cement, feathering the edges so they're smooth. Allow to dry, then apply another coat of joint cement a couple of inches beyond the first coat. Feather the edges and let dry overnight. You can then sand and paint. Fiberglass tape is somewhat similar in application— just follow the directions on the package you buy.

Sand even.

Sand along crack.

Apply joint cement.

Apply tape.

Apply wider coat of cement.

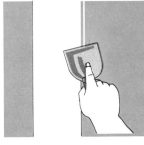

Feather edges.

Stuff newspaper
into hole (above).

Fill with spackle (at right).

Apply final coat of spackle
to surface (below).

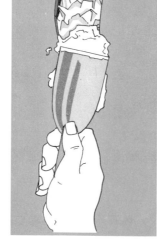

Chip away loose plaster.

Fill part way to surface.

Apply plaster up to
wall surface.

"Cut" surface with steel wool
to give new paint firm hold.

A hole in wallboard can be repaired by plugging it with a wad of newspaper and then using spackle to fill in until you have a flat surface that can be sanded even. It may take a couple of coats of spackle to do the job properly.

Plaster is repaired in much the same manner as wallboard. With cracks more than ¼-inch wide, chip away the loose plaster and wet down the area. Fill it half way to the surface with plaster and let it dry. Then wet it again and apply another coat to the surface of the wall. When it is dry, spackle where needed and sand.

After repairs are completed, clean the surface of dirt and grease. A dry rag or mop will remove dust and some dirt. You may have to wash the surface with a household cleanser to remove stubborn dirt or grease.

Kitchen walls and ceilings usually become covered with a film of grease (which may extend to the walls and ceilings just outside the entrances to the kitchen), and bathroom walls and ceilings may have steamed-on dirt. The grease or dirt must be removed—new paint will not adhere to it. To remove grease or dirt, wash the surface with a strong household cleanser, turpentine, or mineral spirits.

The finish on kitchen and bathroom walls and ceilings is usually a gloss or semigloss. This finish must be "cut" so that the new paint can get a firm hold. Washing with a household cleanser or turpentine will dull the gloss, but for best results, rub the surface with fine sandpaper or steel wool. After using sandpaper or steel wool, wipe the surface to remove dust.

PREPARING WOODWORK

Woodwork (windows, doors, and baseboards) usually has a glossy finish. First wash the surface to remove dirt and grease, and then sand it lightly to "cut" the finish.

After sanding, wipe the surface to remove the dust.

You can buy liquid preparations that will soften hard, glossy finishes to provide good adhesion for new paint.

If there are any bare spots in the wood, touch them up with an undercoat or with pigmented shellac before you paint.

PAINT APPLICATION

Use drop cloths or plastic sheeting to protect floors and furniture. Paint the ceiling first. Don't try to paint too wide a strip at a time. The next strip should be started and lapped into the previous one before the previous one dries.

If you are putting two coats on the ceiling, apply the second coat, and "cut in" at the junction with the walls, before you paint the walls.

Remove all electric switch and receptacle plates from the walls to avoid smearing. Use a cardboard or metal shield to avoid smearing the trim if the trim is to be another color. Or you can use masking tape if you prefer. Wipe spills up immediately.

Start painting a wall at the upper left-hand corner and work down toward the floor (left-handed persons may find it more convenient to start at the upper right-hand corner).

When using a roller, paint over a section of wall about 3 feet wide in a "W" pattern. Fill in the W with horizontal strokes of the roller. Then smooth out with vertical strokes in one direction.

Paint the woodwork last—preferably after the walls are dry.

Flush doors can be painted with a roller. On paneled doors, some parts can be painted with a roller, but other sections require a brush. (You may prefer your doors and other trim in natural color. See below.)

Lap paint over previous strip of paint.

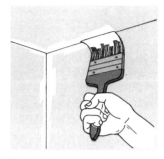

Cut in ceiling-wall joints before you paint the walls.

Remove receptacle plates.

Use a shield to protect trim.

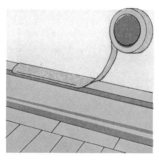

Masking tape to protect trim.

Paint a "W" pattern.

Fill in the "W", then smooth out with vertical strokes.

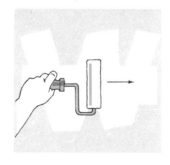

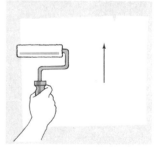

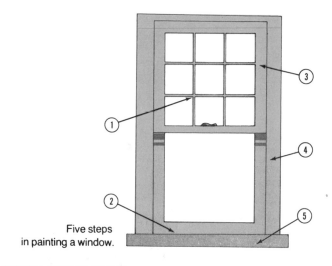

Five steps
in painting a window.

Protecting a window with
masking tape.

Protecting glass
with newspaper.

Soak brushes in
thinner (left).

Work bristles against
side of can (below left).

Squeeze brush between
fingers (below).

Paint the parts of a window in this order: mullions, horizontals of sash, verticals of sash, verticals of frame, horizontal frame, and sill. Windows are easier to paint and to clean afterward if the glass is masked. Both masking tape and liquid masking are available at hardware and paint stores.

A simple way to protect the glass is to cover it with a piece of wet newspaper. The moisture will paste the newspaper to the glass and also prevent paint from soaking into the absorbent paper. When you strip the paper from the glass after painting, the paint will come with it.

CLEANUP

Brushes, rollers, and other equipment should be cleaned as soon as possible after being used.

Equipment used to apply latex paint can be cleaned easily with soap and water. Rinse thoroughly.

Equipment used to apply oil-base paint may be a little harder to clean. Soak brushes in turpentine or thinner long enough to loosen the paint. Then work the bristles against the side and bottom of the container to release the paint. To release the paint in the center of the brush, squeeze or work the bristles between the thumb and forefinger. Rinse the brush in the turpentine or thinner again, and, if necessary, wash it in mild soap suds. Rinse in clear water.

NATURAL FINISHES FOR TRIM

Some doors, particularly flush doors, are attractive in their natural finish. However, they will become discolored and soiled easily unless protected. Your paint dealer can offer suggestions on how to finish and protect your doors. Many kinds of products

Draw design on textured paint.

Fill impressions with deeper color.

are now on the market, and new ones are constantly appearing.

The first step in finishing doors is to obtain the proper color tone. This is usually acquired by staining. Sometimes, however, no staining is required—the preservative finish is enough to bring out the desired color tone. With new doors, you can experiment on the trimmings or shavings to help you make a decision.

The next step is sealing. One coat of shellac is usually adequate. When the shellac is dry, the surface should be sanded smooth, wiped free of dust, and varnished. Rubbing the surface with linseed oil, as is done in furniture finishing, provides a nice soft finish but requires more work. Also, surfaces so finished collect dust more readily.

For a natural finish of other interior trim, you need to specify the desired kind and grade of wood at the time of construction. This can add substantially to the construction costs. If you already have handsome naturally finished woodwork in your home, consider yourself fortunate. And make sure you think twice, then twice more, before painting over it.

UNUSUAL EFFECTS

The beauty of paint lies in its adaptability to your decorating whims. How about textured paint to give your room a new personality? This treatment adds depth to the walls, and its rough finish blends beautifully with various decors. In addition, the heavy consistency of textured paint fills small holes and cracks, making it the perfect camouflage for old, scarred walls that would normally require replastering.

While the paint is still wet, create a random pattern by going over the surface with a special roller, a whisk broom, a comb, or other object that will make a design. Decorators often give a textured finish an individual touch by drawing stylized birds, plants, and other figures and designs. You, too, can do it. Simply draw freehand an outline of whatever you choose, using an unsharpened pencil or similar object. If you wish to make the impressions more outstanding, fill them in with a slightly deeper color when dry.

Striping is another fashionable wall treatment. Paint the walls in the chosen back-

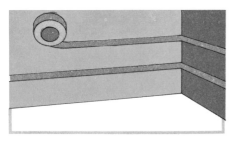

Masking walls
for striping.

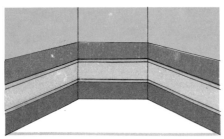

Stripe effect.

Stippling a wall.

ground color and let them dry. Then, using masking tape (which must be securely fastened to the surface), mark off the areas to be striped in the desired widths. Paint these

designated areas in a contrasting color. Let dry thoroughly, then remove the strips of masking tape. The walls are no longer a backdrop; they are one of the most exciting features in the room. Striped walls do wonders to increase the visual size of a small room.

Stippling the walls produces a very decorative effect and gives them dimension. Paint the walls the background color and let dry completely. Then, using a stippling roller (available in a wide assortment of design-producing sleeves), go over the dry walls in a contrasting color of your choice.

Painting Tips

• Do the painting when the room temperature is comfortable for work—between 60 and 70 degrees F. Provide good cross-ventilation both to shorten the drying time and to remove fumes and odors.

• Check the label on the paint can for any special application and drying instructions.

• Preferably, remove all furnishings from the room. Otherwise, cover the furniture, fixtures, and floor with drop cloths or newspapers. No matter how careful you may be, you will spill, drip, or splatter some paint.

• Remove all light switch and wall plug plates. If you wish, paint the plates before you replace them after painting the room.

• Dip your brush into the paint no more than one-third the length of the bristles. This will minimize splattering and dripping.

• When using latex paint, wash your brush or roller occasionally with water. A buildup of the quick-drying paint in the nap of the roller or at the base of the bristles of the brush can cause excessive dripping.

• Wipe up spilled, splattered, or dripped paint as you go along. Paint is easier to clean up when it is wet.

• Do not let the paint dry out in the can or in brushes or rollers between jobs or during long interruptions in a job. After each job, replace the can lid securely, and clean brushes or rollers. During long interruptions in a job, also replace the can lid, and either clean brushes or rollers or suspend them in water.

Safety Tips

• Never paint in a completely closed room, and use caution when painting in a room where there is an open flame or fire. Some paints give off fumes that are flammable or dangerous to breathe or both.

• Avoid prolonged exposure to paint fumes for a day or two after painting. Such fumes can also be harmful to canaries or other pet birds.

• Use a sturdy stepladder or other support when painting high places. Be sure that the ladder is positioned firmly, with the legs fully opened and locked in position (see CHAPTER 4).

• Face the ladder when climbing up or down it, holding on with at least one hand. Lean toward the ladder when painting.

• Do not overreach when painting. Move the ladder frequently rather than risk a fall. And, to avoid spilling the paint, take the few seconds required to remove the paint can from the ladder before you move it.

• When you finish painting, dispose of used rags by putting them in a covered metal can. If left lying around, the oily rags could catch fire by spontaneous combustion.

• Store paint in a safe, but well-ventilated, place where children and pets cannot get to it. A locked cabinet is ideal if well ventilated. Unless needed for retouching, small quantities of paint may not be worth saving.

If You Have the Painting Done

You may prefer to have all or part of your painting done by a professional painter. When you hire a contractor, it is a good idea to get a signed agreement specifying:

• The specific price for the job.

• Exactly what areas or surfaces are to be painted.

• The types, brands, and quality of paints to be used and the number of coats, including primer coats, to be applied.

• The measures to be taken to protect floors, furnishings, and other parts of the house.

• A complete cleanup guarantee.

• A completion date (allowing for possible delays—because of bad weather, for example).

Check the contractor's work with friends or neighbors who may have hired him in the past. Be sure that he is fully insured (Workmen's Compensation and Employer's Liability Insurance, Public Liability, and Property Damage Insurance). Otherwise, you could be held liable for accidents that occurred on your property.

6

Exterior Painting

Some people enjoy painting the house; for others it's a chore. But it must be done occasionally. One reason is for appearance. An even more important one is for protection of the wood or other surface.

When repainting is needed, delay can mean extra work when you finally do paint. Old paint that blisters, cracks, and peels must be removed before new paint can be applied.

If you wait too long, there could be costly damage. Wood rots when not fully protected. Also, moisture is allowed to reach the interior, where it can cause damage. Some metals rust when not protected; others develop a corrosive wash that stains surrounding surfaces.

On the other hand, too-frequent repainting builds up an excessively thick film that is more sensitive to the deteriorating effects of the weather. Ordinarily, every four years is often enough to repaint a house. Sheltered areas, such as eaves and porch ceilings, may not need repainting every time the body of the house is repainted; every other time may be sufficient.

Take the time and effort to do a good job when you paint. First, use good-quality paint. It will give longer and better protection. Second, prepare the surface properly. Even the best paint won't last on a poorly prepared surface. You will be wasting your time and money.

Calk joints tightly.

SURFACE PREPARATION

In general, a surface that is to be painted should be firm, smooth, and clean. With oil-base paint, it must also be dry. Latex or water-base paint can be applied to a damp surface (but not to a wet one). The paint-can label may contain additional or special instructions for preparing the surface.

Apply calking compound around windows and doors and wherever dissimilar materials abut (wood–masonry, wood–metal, wood siding–trim, etc.). Tightly calked joints helped to weatherproof your house and prevent moisture seepage with its subsequent damage to paint film.

WOOD SURFACES

Wood siding preferably should not contain knots or sappy streaks. But if new siding does, clean the knots and streaks with turpentine and seal with a good knot sealer. The knot sealer will seal in oily extractives and prevent staining and cracking of the paint.

Smooth any rough spots in the wood with sandpaper or other abrasive. Dust the surface just before you paint it.

Old surfaces in good condition—just slightly faded, dirty, or chalky—may need only dusting before being repainted. Very dirty surfaces should be washed with a mild detergent and rinsed thoroughly with water. Grease or other oily matter may be removed with mineral spirits.

Remove all nail rust marks. Set nailheads below the surface, prime them, and putty the holes. Fasten loose siding with galvanized or other nonrusting nails. Fill all cracks; compounds for that purpose are available from paint and hardware stores. Sand smooth after the compound dries.

Remove all rough, loose, flaking, and blistering paint. Spot-prime the bare spots before repainting. If the cracking or blistering of the old paint extends over a large area, remove all old paint down to bare wood. Prime and repaint the old surface as you would a new wood surface. Sand or ''feather'' the edges of the sound paint before you repaint.

Before you repaint, be sure to correct the condition that caused the blistering, cracking, or peeling of the old paint. Otherwise, you may run into the same trouble again. It

1. Seal knots so they won't show through paint.

2. Set nailheads below surface.

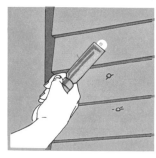

3. Fill holes with putty.

4. Fill cracks in siding.

5. Spot-prime before painting.

6. Feather edges of sound paint.

may be a moisture problem. See CHAPTER 7 for causes and cures.

Old paint may be removed by sanding, scraping, or burning, or with chemical paint

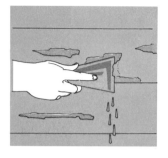

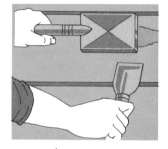

Scraping old paint from rough surfaces (above).

Sanding smooth surfaces (above right).

Using an electric paint softener (right).

METAL SURFACES

New galvanized steel surfaces (such as gutters and leaders) should weather for about 6 months before being painted. If earlier painting is necessary, first wash the surface with a vinegar solution and rinse it thoroughly. This will remove any manufacturing residue and stain inhibitors. Apply a special primer before painting.

Rust and loose paint can usually be removed from old surfaces with sandpaper or with a stiff wire brush. Chipping may be necessary in severe cases. Chemical rust removers are available.

Oil and grease may be removed with a solvent such as mineral spirits. Rinse the surface thoroughly.

remover. Scraping is the simplest but hardest method. Sanding is most effective on smooth surfaces. Chemical paint remover can be expensive for large areas. Only experienced persons should attempt burning. An electric paint softener is much safer.

MASONRY SURFACES

New concrete should weather for several months before being painted. If earlier painting is necessary, first wash the surface with a solvent such as mineral spirits to remove oil or grease. Fresh concrete may contain considerable moisture and alkali, so it is best to paint with latex paints.

Patch any cracks or other defects in masonry surfaces. Pay particular attention to mortar joints. Mortar and concrete patching compounds are available at hardware stores. Follow label directions for use.

Clean both new and old surfaces thor-

Patch masonry cracks (left).

Replace crumbling mortar (below).

Wire-brushing masonry surface (below right).

oughly before painting. Remove dirt, loose particles, and efflorescence with a wire brush. Oil and grease may be removed by washing the surface with a commercial cleanser or with a detergent and water. Loose, peeling, or heavily chalked paint may be removed by sandblasting. This is normally a professional operation.

If the old paint is just moderately chalked but is otherwise "tight" and nonflaking, coat it with a recommended sealer or conditioner before you repaint with a water-base paint. Some latex paints are modified to allow painting over slightly chalked surfaces. Follow the manufacturer's directions for use.

After cleaning the surface, wash or hose it—unless efflorescence was present.

PAINT APPLICATION METHODS

Exterior paint may be applied by brush, roller, or spray. You can paint faster with a roller than with a brush; however, a brush may give better penetration on wood surfaces. With a roller, you still need a brush for "cutting in." This means extra tools to clean after the job is finished.

Rollers work well on masonry and metal surfaces. Proper depth of the pile on the roller cover is important and varies from one surface to another. Follow the manufacturer's recommendations.

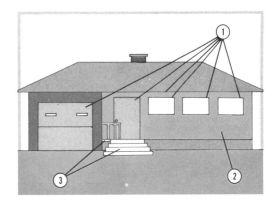

House painting sequence:
1-Windows, trim, doors;
2-Body of house;
3-Porches, steps.

Spraying is the fastest method. But you may not get proper penetration on wood surfaces. On masonry surfaces, voids that are difficult to fill with a brush or roller can be coated adequately by spraying. Surrounding surfaces must be well protected when spray-painting.

Paint the windows, trim, and doors before you paint the body of the house. Paint wood porches and steps last.

Read the paint-can label carefully before you start to paint. It will contain specific directions for application.

WHEN TO PAINT

New wood should be painted promptly (within two weeks) after its installation. If you find that this cannot be done, it is advantageous to protect the bare wood as soon as possible against the entrance of rain and heavy dew and mildew by brushing a paintable water-repellent preservative solution on the siding, trim, and into all joints.

Spray-painting masonry
is the fastest method.

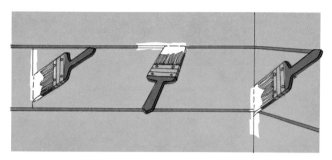

Brush into all joints.

Wood so treated should be allowed to dry for a few days prior to painting or staining.

The best time to paint is during clear, dry weather. Temperatures must be above 50 degrees F. Latex paints may be applied even though the surface to be painted is damp from condensation or rain. Solvent-thinned paints should be applied only to a dry surface.

If the outside temperature is high (70 degrees F. or higher), it is best to paint those surfaces already reached by shade. This is known as "following the sun around the house." To avoid the wrinkling and flatting of solvent-thinned paints, and water marks on latex paints, do not paint late in the day in early spring or late fall when heavy dew is common.

Do not paint in windy or dusty weather or when insects may get caught in the paint. Insects are usually the biggest problem during fall evenings. Don't try to remove insects from wet paint; brush them off after the paint dries.

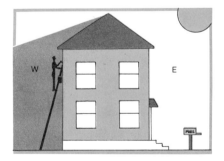

"Following the sun around the house."

HOW MANY COATS?

For the original paint job on new wood surfaces, three coats are recommended. A three-coat system will perform better and last much longer than a two-coat job. However, most original paint jobs are two-coat applications. If you plan to limit yours to two coats, be certain to apply both generously, toward the lower spreading rate of the range specified by the manufacturer on the label of the container. Again, manufacturer's instructions for use of primer and topcoat should be followed. On factory-primed sidings, the factory primer will take the place of one of the required coats.

Repaint work is best limited to a single coat of topcoat paint of a similar color. If you plan a color change, two coats of topcoat paint may be required. If bare wood is exposed, areas should be spot-primed before the topcoat paint is applied.

Use a good-quality oil-base exterior primer with solvent-thinned paint. Most manufacturers recommend use of a solvent-thinned primer with latex or water-base paint. A solvent-thinned primer may be applied to a dry surface only. Prime after you clean and repair the surface, but before you putty cracks or other defects.

Allow the primer coat to dry according to the manufacturer's label instructions. Allow longer drying time in humid weather. Apply the finish coats as soon as the primer has dried sufficiently. Allow about 48 hours' drying time between oil-base finish coats. Two coats of latex paint may be applied in one day.

On metal surfaces, prime both new metal and old metal from which the paint has been removed. Good primers usually contain zinc dust, red lead, zinc yellow, blue lead, iron oxide, or some rust-inhibiting pigment as one of the ingredients. After the primer has dried sufficiently, apply one or two finish coats of paint.

Chapter 6 • Exterior Painting

PUTTING ON THE PAINT

Stir or shake oil-base paint thoroughly before you start to paint. Stir it frequently while painting. Latex or water-base paint should not be shaken—it foams.

If you are using a gallon of paint, transfer it to a larger container or pour about half into another container. It will be easier to handle, and there will be room to dip the brush.

Dip your brush about one-third the length of the bristles. Tap off excess paint on the inside of the can; do not scrape the brush across the rim.

On windows, paint the wood dividing the glass first. Then paint the frame, trim, sill, and apron in that order. Shutters and storm sash are easier to paint if removed from the house and laid flat on supports. Wipe off dust and dirt before painting them.

On siding, start painting at a high point of the house—at a corner or under the eave. Paint from top to bottom. Complete one sidewall before starting another.

Paint along the grain of the wood. If you are painting with a brush, use long sweeping arm strokes, keeping an even pressure on the brush. Apply both sides of each brushful. End each stroke with a light lifting motion.

Apply paint to an unpainted area and work into the wet edge of the previously painted portion. When you finish an area, go over it with light, quick strokes to smooth brush marks and to recoat any thin spots.

Cleanup after painting is the same as described in CHAPTER 6.

1. Stir oil-base paint.

2. Pour into another container.

3. Dip your brush.

RIGHT

WRONG

4. Tap off excess paint—do not scrape bristles.

5. Start at a high point.

6. Paint along the grain.

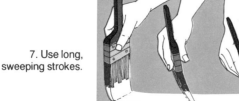

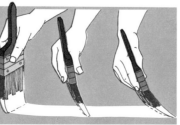

7. Use long, sweeping strokes.

8. Work into the previously painted area.

NATURAL FINISHES

Natural finishes help to retain or enhance the natural color and grain of wood. Such finishes are most extensively used on the more attractive siding woods such as redwood, western red cedar, and Philippine mahogany but are not limited to use on these species. They are relatively easy to apply and economical to maintain. The natural-finish family includes water-repellent preservatives, bleaches, and penetrating or semitransparent stains. All are either unpigmented (clear) or pigmented very slightly, hence the term "natural finishes."

Paintable water-repellent preservatives (WRP) repel liquids such as rainwater and dew and thereby reduce the swelling and shrinking of wood. They also protect wood against mildew and decay.

The WRPs are easy to apply by brush or roller, or by dipping the wood before installation. They penetrate wood, leaving its appearance relatively unchanged except for an initial slight darkening reaction. Treatment with WRP slows the weathering process and protects against water staining as well as mildew.

Where paintable water-repellent preservative is the sole treatment to be applied to exterior wood surfaces, two coats are recommended. The best results are obtained when the first coat is applied to the back, face, edges, and ends of the wood before it is nailed into place. After installation, the second coat should be brushed over all exposed wood surfaces. As weathering progresses, the color of WRP-treated wood may lighten.

The frequency with which the water-repellent preservative needs to be renewed is dependent upon climatic conditions. In relatively dry areas, the treatment retains its effectiveness longer than in areas subject to extensive rainfall, and it may not need to be renewed for three to five years.

Checking to see if WRP is still effective.

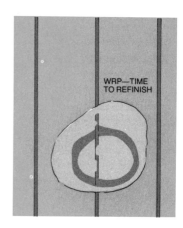

Where the treated wood is subject to frequent wetting, renewal may be required after 12 to 18 months. Successive retreatment may be extended to two years or more. Darkening of the wood or the appearance of blotchy discoloration are indications that the treatment has lost its effectiveness. This may be verified by splashing half a cup of water against the treated wood surface. If the water balls up and runs off, the treatment is still effective. If the water soaks quickly into the wood, it is time to refinish. A single recoat should suffice.

Some homeowners want their houses to have a weathered appearance sooner than natural weathering provides. This can be achieved by applying a bleach or bleaching oil. Bleaching oils are available in many paint stores. In addition to a bleaching chemical, the better bleaching oils contain pigments to impart a grayed appearance to wood and an agent to protect the finish against mildew.

By means of chemical reaction with the wood, bleaches hasten the natural color changes brought on by weathering and eliminate the darkening that often occurs when wood weathers naturally. On new wood, two coats of bleach are recommended. The original application is often the last. Reapplication of bleach is required only if the wood begins to darken or if the bleaching becomes uneven.

Since the bleaching action is aided by moisture, together with sunlight, it is helpful to spray bleached surfaces periodically with water from the garden hose.

Semitransparent stains, sometimes called penetrating stains, contain a small amount of pigment that allows them to alter the natural color of wood but only partially obscure the grain or texture. They are generally offered in natural wood-tone colors and are available in either solvent-thinned or water-thinned types.

Two coats of penetrating stain are generally recommended on new wood, and application is best done by brush or flat applicator. Roller or spray application, followed by brushing, may be used on smooth wood and textured surfaces. Care should be taken on windy, dry days to avoid lap marks due to fast absorption.

Penetrating stains leave a flat or dull finish. They are a "breathing" type of finish, since they do not form a continuous film or coating on the surface of the wood. A penetrating stain finish is gradually worn away by the weather. When the erosion progresses to the point that portions of the wood show through, it is time to refinish. A single refinish coat is generally adequate.

SOLID-COLOR STAINS

The increasing use of textured wood sidings, an ideal surface for stains, has added to the popularity of solid-color stains. Also called heavy-bodied stains, they are made with a much higher concentration of pigment than penetrating stains. As a result, solid-color stains have higher hiding power, sufficiently high to obscure the natural color and grain of wood. They are more like paint than stain.

As a rule, only a single coat of solid-color stain is applied, but two coats provide better and longer service. Any of the conventional methods of application may be used to apply the stain to smooth wood surfaces, but brush application is best.

7

Paint Failure
—Causes and Cures

THERE ARE FEW things more discouraging than giving your home a lovely new paint job, then watching it deteriorate before your eyes. It is especially frustrating if you've bought good paint, used good tools, and taken pains preparing the surface. What went wrong? Assuming you've followed all the instructions to the letter, how could it all crumble away in a few months, or a year? The answer is often traceable to one primary cause—moisture, a menace to the best of paint jobs.

INTERIOR FAILURE

The paint, preparation, and application have all been the best. Why do the ceilings peel, the walls blister? It will probably pay to have a plumber check for leakage somewhere in the water supply or sewage systems. Just a tiny leak can have a devastat-

Blistering, peeling wall (at left).

Scrape away all damaged paint (below left).

Install a hood and fan above range (below).

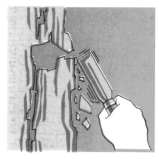

ing effect upon the surrounding walls. Moisture in the plaster causes blistering, peeling, and eventual ruination of the entire wall. If you suspect a leak behind the wall, no matter how slight, by all means have it corrected.

Ceilings, of course, can be ruined in the same manner, but many times the affected area is confined to that part of the ceiling which is underneath a toilet, tub, or washbasin. Frequent spillage of water from these sources seeps into the plaster or wallboard and causes moisture difficulties that are difficult to eradicate. Sometimes a more moisture-resistant floor overhead (ceramic tile, for example) will help, though this solution may require extensive and expensive structural modifications.

Even after you have sealed off the moisture source, the trouble may persist, because the dampness stays in the plaster or wallboard for a long time after the original soaking. This can usually be overcome by using an aluminum paint under a primer. If care is taken to scrape all affected paint from the surface, and the directions on the label of the aluminum paint are carefully followed, the problem should be solved.

Often paint cracks and peels above a kitchen range. The cure is a range hood with a fan to draw off the hot, moist vapors.

EXTERIOR PAINT BREAKDOWNS

More serious problems occur in exterior paint. There are many types of failure and as many causes.

Blistering occurs when moisture trapped in siding is drawn from the wood by exposure to the sun and pushes paint from the surface. First you must find and eliminate sources of moisture. Is there seepage or leakage from eaves, roofs, or plumbing? Is the area near a a bathroom or kitchen? Consider installing moisture-escape devices such as louvers, exhaust fans, or vents.

Scrape off old paint around the blistered area. Sanu the surface to bare wood and spot-prime with an undercoat. Seal all seams, holes, and cracks against moisture with calking compound. Apply a topcoat of quality house paint according to the directions on the label.

Chalking is normal, and even desirable, since it keeps paint clean. But when paint chalks excessively, it will not last long. The cure: be more generous with paint. Don't spread it too thin. Use two coats. Use chalk-retardant paints above masonry.

Flaking or chalking paint on masonry surfaces is caused by inadequate surface preparation. The paint flakes off in "scales" or powders and chalks off. The solution is first to remove flaking and chalking paint by wire-brushing. Seal all surface cracks against moisture with concrete patch. Apply a masonry conditioner according to the manufacturer's directions, then apply two topcoats of latex house paint or exterior masonry paint.

Cracking and alligatoring usually indicate that paint was applied in several heavy

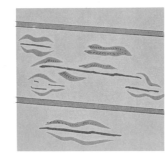

Blistered siding.

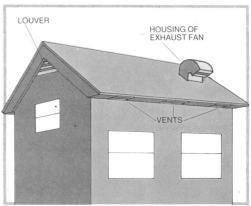

Install louvers, vents, exhaust fans.

Seal seams, cracks.

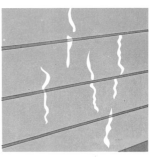

Excessive chalking.

Flaking, chalking on masonry.

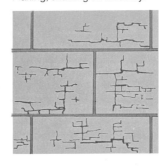

Cracking and alligatoring.

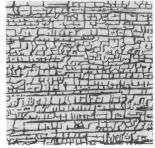

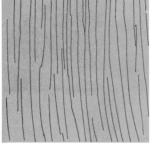

Checking.

Fill primed cracks.

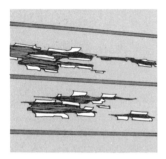

Peeling.

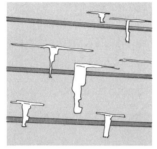

Flaking.

Topcoat peeling on overhanging horizontal surfaces.

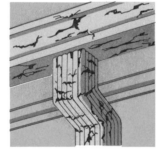

Peeling, cracking on metal surfaces.

coats without sufficient drying time between coats, or that the undercoat used was not compatible with the finish coat. Sand the cracked or alligatored surface smooth. Then apply one coat of undercoat and one topcoat of recommended quality house paint according to label directions.

Checking is most commonly found on plywood veneer and is caused by expansion and contraction as it weathers and ages. To correct the problem, sand the surface smooth. If the cracked area is not extensive, spot-prime the exposed bare wood with an exterior undercoat. Fill primed cracks with calking compound. Apply a topcoat of recommended quality paint.

Should the problem be extensive, the best procedure is to replace the plywood. To prevent the problem on new plywood, sand the surface smooth, then apply one coat of latex wood primer and two coats of quality latex house paint according to label directions.

Peeling, like blistering, is caused when moisture trapped in siding is drawn from the wood by the sun's heat and pushes paint from the surface. The solution is to find and eliminate sources of moisture, following the same procedures as for blistering. Then scrape and repaint.

Flaking occurs when siding alternately swells and shrinks as moisture from behind it is absorbed and then dries out. The brittle paint film cracks under the strain and pulls away from the wood. Corrective measures are the same as for blistering.

Topcoat peeling is usually found on overhanging horizontal surfaces and other areas protected from the weather. It is caused by poor adhesion to the previous coat of paint because built-up salt deposits have not been washed away by rain. Sand the surface thoroughly to remove all peeling paint. Wash the sanded surface with a solution of three heaping tablespoons of trisodium phosphate to one gallon of water. Rinse well and allow to dry. Apply one coat of undercoat and one topcoat of quality house paint according to label directions.

Peeling or cracking of paint on galvanized metal gutters and downspouts indicates the use of improper metal primer or no primer at all. The paint film has little or no adhesion. Strip off all loose paint by scraper, wire brush, or power wire-brushing. It is very important that all loose paint be removed, or succeeding coats of paint will subsequently peel away too. When finishing with oil-base topcoat, prime bare spots with a metal primer. When finishing with latex topcoat, apply latex paint directly to bare galvanized areas after cleaning with a solvent and allowing the solvent to evaporate.

Fading is normal, but if it is excessive, salt air from the seashore is very often the cause. Sometimes heavy pounding of wind-driven rain or snow, followed by bright sunlight, will cause one side of the house to fade more quickly than the others. Not much can be done about it, but be sure to buy the best brand of paint, since it will invariably contain more and better pigment than cheaper types and thus hold out a bit longer.

Bleeding sometimes occurs on redwood and cedar siding and shingles. Sap runs or bleeds through paint and stains the surface. It is caused by inadequate sealing at the first paint application. If shake/shingle paints don't do the trick, the cure may be drastic. Stained areas may have to be scraped to raw wood and coated with knot sealer. If the staining material is creosote from an earlier application, the stain is blotchy rather than runny. Scraping down to bare wood is then the only cure. It's a tough one, but it can be done.

Mildew thrives on high humidity and high temperature, which stimulate fungus growth on paint film. If left on the surface and painted over, it will grow through the new coat of paint. The cure is to scrub the entire surface with a solution of one-third cup of trisodium phosphate and eight tablespoons of household bleach in four quarts of warm water. Then apply a wood undercoat. Mildew-resistant additive may be added to the undercoat if mildew conditions are severe and an oil-base topcoat is used. The additive in a finish coat should be avoided. The topcoat should be a quality mildew-resistant house paint.

Staining occurs when moisture in the siding dissolves coloring matter in the wood. Colored water escapes onto the surface through breaks in the paint film and drips from underneath overlapping boards. Stain is deposited as the water dries. The solution is first to find and eliminate sources of moisture. Then wash the stained surface with a mixture of 50 percent denatured alcohol and 50 percent clean water. Allow the surface to dry for 48 hours. Then apply two coats of quality house paint.

Excessive moisture may cause rusting of

Rusting nails.

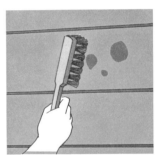

Wire-brush stained area.

Bleeding.

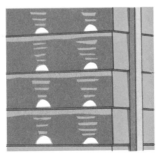

Mildew.

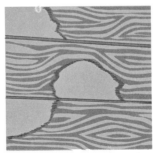

Staining.

uncoated steel nails used in construction. After finding and eliminating sources of moisture, sand or wire-brush the stained paint and remove rust down to the bright

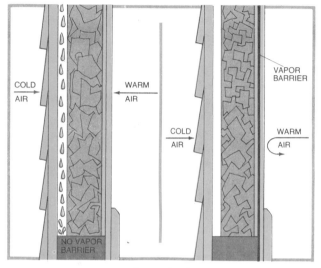

A vapor barrier protects against blistering and peeling, whereas the lack of one lets the water condensation run to the bottom of the wall.

metal of the nailhead. Countersink the nailhead ⅛ inch below the surface of the siding. Immediately spot-prime the nailhead with undercoat. Fill the countersunk hole with calking compound or putty (see CHAPTER 6). Apply two coats of quality house paint according to label directions.

STRUCTURAL PROBLEMS

Insulated homes are certainly desirable, but they pose problems for the painter. If a home is insulated without a proper vapor barrier between the warm side of the house and the insulating material, water vapor condenses and runs between studs to the bottom of the wall, causing severe paint blistering and peeling. There is no real cure for this except to tear the walls apart and start over, which seems a bit drastic. It may be helpful to use latex paints.

Another trouble spot might be a crawl space. Moisture is often generated in these areas, then travels up through the walls, causing paint problems inside as well as out. Again, latex paint may help, but a more permanent cure may be needed.

Adequate ventilation is essential. There

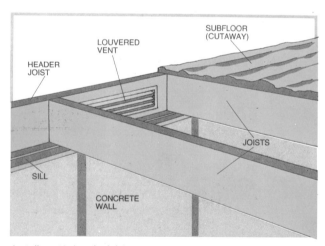

Install vent in header joist.

Install vent in place of one block of concrete-block foundation.

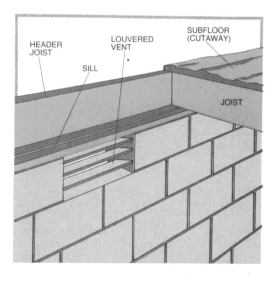

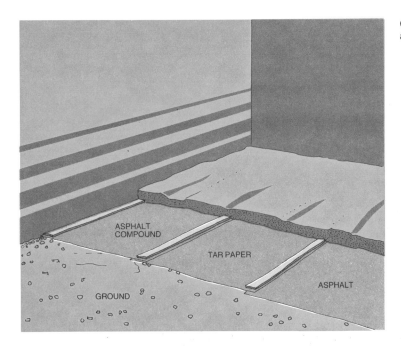

Cover ground with tar paper and spread layer of sand over it.

ASPHALT COMPOUND

TAR PAPER

ASPHALT

GROUND

should be vents or louvers on at least two opposite sides of the crawl space to provide cross-ventilation. If necessary, you can install vents by cutting holes through the header joists. If the foundation is of concrete block, you can simply knock out a block to emplace a vent. Louvered vents, which can be closed off in wet or cold weather, are best. Most of them are also screened to keep out rodents and other small animals.

If dampness persists, cover the ground in the crawl space with heavy tarpaper. Overlap the joints 3 to 4 inches, and seal them with asphalt compound. Seal the tarpaper to the foundation walls with the compound. Then spread a 2-inch layer of dry sand over the tarpaper. This should solve the problem permanently.

Siding on ground-hugging houses, such as those built on concrete slabs, is sometimes in contact with the ground, drawing up moisture and causing peeling. (It also serves as an open invitation to invasion by termites.) Again, latex paint may help the

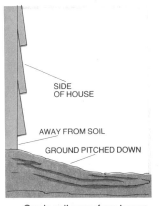

SIDE OF HOUSE

AWAY FROM SOIL

GROUND PITCHED DOWN

Grade soil away from house.

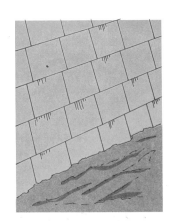

Siding in contact with ground.

peeling problem. A more permanent solution would be to regrade to eliminate the siding-ground contact. But make sure that the pitch of the soil is away from the house. Otherwise, you will be trading a headache for a migraine.

Paint Failure—Causes and Cures • Chapter 7

8

Wallpapering

THE SPECIAL EFFECTS that can be achieved and the seemingly endless varieties of handsome patterns reflecting just about any mood make wallpaper a valuable asset in the home or apartment owner's decorating portfolio. The term wallpaper, it should be noted, does not apply exclusively to paper substances that are hung on a wall. It also includes vinyls, foils, grass cloth, fabrics, cork, and many other wallcovering materials available from your wallpaper dealer.

Wallpapering can be done with professional results by almost anyone willing to plan carefully and work slowly. It is not a difficult task, but it does require patience. Wallpaper can be purchased pretrimmed and prepasted so that all you have to do is soak it in water and apply it to the walls while wet. Hanging regular wallpaper, which must be trimmed and pasted, is not much harder to do.

The selection of wallpaper color and pattern is largely a matter of personal preference. Books and magazines about interior decorating are full of ideas regarding the use of wallpaper. In addition, many wallpaper dealers can give you valuable advice about how to achieve different effects—brightening a room or wall, visually lengthening a room, and coordinating carpet and furniture colors and styles.

The selection of wallpaper material is partly a matter of function. Vinyl wallcoverings should certainly be used in kitchens, bathrooms, hallways, or other areas where exposure to moisture and the elements could create a problem. It is extremely durable and moisture- and grease-resistant. In an entryway, durability is not a major consideration, but dramatic appearance may be. Foils, flocks, or grass cloth can be the answer to a decorating problem here. Again, your dealer can help in your choice.

WALLPAPER COLORS AND PATTERNS

The colors in a wallpaper vary slightly between different runs. If you have to reorder wallpaper, there is a good chance that the new order will not color-match the previous lot. Therefore, estimate your needs carefully and order enough wallpaper at one time to complete your entire job.

Blank stock is an unpatterned wallpaper commonly applied to a wall to provide a smooth surface for foil wallpaper and other special applications. All other wallpaper is patterned.

Some patterns—many of the vertical

stripes, for example—require little or no matching. The paper can be cut almost to the exact length required. Since only an inch or two extra length for trimming is needed on each strip, there is very little waste. The same is true of randomly patterned papers such as grass cloth or burlap.

Other patterns can involve considerable waste in installation. A clue to the amount of waste can be gained from the size of the repeat. This information is provided in the wallpaper catalog from which you make your selection. For example, the catalog may state that a certain pattern is repeated every 19 inches. Assume that the distance between the baseboard and the ceiling of the room that you want to paper is 94 inches. The 19-inch pattern will go into the 94-inch wall 5 times — with 1 inch left over for trimming. This pattern would result in very little waste.

You may find that another pattern is repeated every 18 inches. For the same wall, this pattern would repeat 6 times with 14 inches left over. The 18-inch pattern results in 14 inches of trim waste required for each strip. Unless you can find a place to use these remnants (over a window or door, for example), you will have a lot of waste.

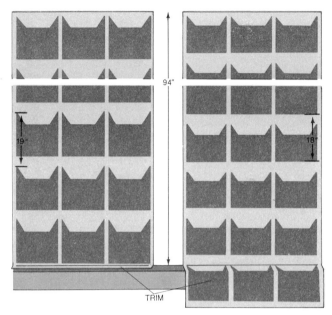

19-inch repeat on 94-inch wall.   18-inch repeat on 94-inch wall.

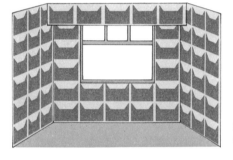

Papering a valance.

ESTIMATING WALLPAPER, TRIM, AND PASTE

Always plan on having some extra wallpaper; it may be needed for several reasons. A strip of wallpaper may be ruined in handling and need replacement. Other surfaces in a room (valances, for example) may be included in the job and require additional wallpaper. Future repairs may become necessary for which it is important to have wallpaper of the original batch. The same wallpaper, if bought later, may not exactly match the color of that on your wall.

The amount of wallpaper required to cover a surface depends not only on the size of the surface but on the wallpaper pattern as well. To make your estimate, you should know a few facts about wallpaper. It is sold in a variety of widths. Regardless of width, each single roll has 36 square feet of wallpaper (double rolls are also available). The length of each roll depends upon the width. The wider the roll, the shorter the length, and therefore fewer individual strips can be cut from the roll for hanging. When estimating the amount of wallpaper needed, count on about 30 square feet of coverage per roll, allowing 6 square feet for

WALLPAPER ESTIMATING CHART

Distance around room in feet	Single rolls for wall areas Height of ceiling			Number yards for borders	Single rolls for ceilings
	8 feet	9 feet	10 feet		
28	8	8	10	11	2
30	8	8	10	11	2
32	8	10	10	12	2
34	10	10	12	13	4
36	10	10	12	13	4
38	10	12	12	14	4
40	10	12	12	15	4
42	12	12	14	15	4
44	12	12	14	16	4
46	12	14	14	17	6
48	14	14	16	17	6
50	14	14	16	18	6
52	14	14	16	19	6
54	14	16	18	19	6
56	14	16	18	20	8
58	16	16	18	21	8
60	16	18	20	21	8
62	16	18	20	22	8
64	16	18	20	23	8
66	18	20	20	23	10
68	18	20	22	24	10
70	18	20	22	25	10
72	18	20	22	25	12
74	20	22	22	26	12
76	20	22	24	27	12
78	20	22	24	27	14
80	20	22	26	28	14
82	22	24	26	29	14
84	22	24	26	30	16
86	22	24	26	30	16
88	24	26	28	31	16
90	24	26	28	32	18

Note: Deduct one single roll for every two ordinary size doors and windows or every 30 square feet of wall opening.

fireplaces, make your estimate for the entire surface. Then reduce your estimate by ⅓ to ½ roll for each door, window, and fireplace, or 10 to 15 square feet each. If you estimate your needs in this way, you should have enough wallpaper to complete the job plus some left over.

You may prefer to have your wallpaper dealer estimate your needs. He is an expert. After you have selected a wallpaper pattern, he can tell you exactly how much you need if you give him sketches and measurements of the room.

The amount of paste needed for paper that is not prepasted depends on the number of rolls and the type of wallpaper you are using. Wheat paste can be used with most types; one pound of dry mix is generally enough to hang six to eight rolls of wallpaper. More dry mix may be needed than is recommended by the label instructions. Following label instructions sometimes results in a paste that is too thin.

Some dry-mix pastes contain mildew-resistant additives. These should always be used with coated vinyl wallpaper. The weight and type of backing on the vinyl determines the amount of adhesive needed. One gallon of vinyl adhesive is generally enough to hang two to four rolls of wallpaper. Ask your wallpaper dealer to recommend the amount and type of adhesive needed for your specific job.

Trim can be used as a decorative border, or to lessen the effects of any sudden change in patterns and colors between ceilings and walls. Trim is sold by the yard. Therefore, when measuring for trim, round off measurements to the next higher yard.

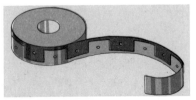
Trim.

waste (allow for greater waste if the repeat requires it). For estimating surfaces that are interrupted by doors, windows, and

VINYLS

The three kinds of vinyl wallpaper commonly available are vinyl laminated to paper, vinyl laminated to cloth, and vinyl-impregnated cloth on paper backing. These vinyl wallpapers are extremely durable. They are easy to clean (scrubbable) and very resistant to damage. Most vinyl wallpapers are nonporous.

Pay close attention to labeling. Some wallpapers are vinyl-coated only. These are not particularly wear-resistant, grease-resistant, or washable. Do not confuse them with vinyl wallpapers.

Before hanging vinyl wallpapers, old paper on the wall should be removed. It is probably glued to the wall with wheat paste. Because vinyls are nonporous, moisture from the adhesive will be sealed in and cause the wheat paste to mildew. Also, sealed-in moisture can soak through old wallpaper and cause it to peel loose from the wall, taking along the vinyl that is pasted over it.

It is recommended that sizing be applied to surfaces before papering with vinyl. Sizing provides a good bonding surface. It also makes it easier to slide wallpaper strips into alignment for matching and making seams. The best sizing is a coat of the same vinyl adhesive you will use for applying the vinyl wallpaper. Be sure that any sizing you use is mildew-resistant.

Use mildew-resistant adhesives only. It is recommended that special vinyl adhesives be used. Paper-backed vinyl sometimes tends to curl back from the wall along edges at seams. Seams can then be difficult to finish. Use of vinyl adhesive prevents this problem.

Vinyl wallpaper stretches if pulled. If it is stretched while being applied, hairline cracks will appear at seams when the wallpaper shrinks as it dries. Be careful, therefore, to avoid stretching vinyl wallpaper.

Some wallpapers find that a squeegee works better than a smoothing brush for smoothing vinyl wallpaper.

FOILS

Foil wallpaper is available either with a simulated metallic finish or as aluminum laminated to paper. All foils must be handled carefully. Do not fold or wrinkle foil, because creases cannot be removed. Because of their reflective surface, foils will magnify any imperfections on the surface to which they are applied. Foils are nonporous; like vinyls, they don't "breathe."

Do not apply a cereal-based sizing to the wall; it could mildew. Sand the wall lightly with Production-grade fine sandpaper to remove texture and imperfections.

It is generally recommended that the surface first be covered with blank stock. This serves two purposes: it helps smooth the surface and it absorbs moisture from the adhesive used for the foil, thus speeding the drying process. Apply blank stock with the same adhesive used for applying the foil.

Use mildew-resistant adhesives only. It is recommended that vinyl adhesives be used because the foil seals the adhesive from the air and drying is retarded. Vinyl adhesives dry relatively fast. Wheat paste could mildew and should never be used with foil.

Some foils must be hung dry. Paste is applied to the wall and the foil is positioned on the paste. Special instructions such as these would come with the wallpaper.

GRASS CLOTH, HEMP, BURLAP, CORK

These materials are generally mounted on a paper backing. The patterns and textures are usually random and require no

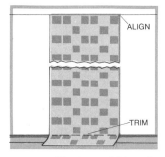

Align top end, trim only at bottom.

Align seams by pushing with the palms of your hands.

Smooth with paint roller.

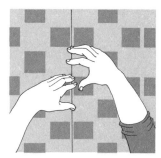

Press seams with fingers.

Blot seams to remove excess paste.

blank stock, you should apply sizing to the wall. Sizing provides a sealed surface that makes it easier to slide the wallpaper into place.

Be careful not to oversoak the backing—it can be weakened and allow the surface to separate. Rather than pasting several strips ahead, paste one strip and hang it before pasting the next strip.

These materials may be difficult to cut when wet. The job of trimming will be easier if you align the top end of the strip to the ceiling and do all the trimming at the bottom end of the strip. Mark it at the baseboard and cut with a scissors.

To align seams, push the wallpaper gently with the palms of your hands. Do not use a smoothing brush; the paper can be damaged by rubbing. Smooth it to the wall with a paint roller. Press seams into place with your fingers—don't use a seam roller, but firm the seams with a soft paint roller. Remove excess paste by wiping gently or blotting with a damp sponge.

In grass cloth, the color will vary slightly between rolls and even from one part of a roll to another. It is a good idea to first cut all full-length strips and arrange them for best appearance. Then stack them in this order for pasting. The edges of grass cloth are sometimes ragged. In this case, you may wish to trim ½ inch off the edges before hanging. This will make a good, sharp edge for seams. For best results, trim the edges after the grass cloth is pasted.

matching. Because of this, there is little waste. When cutting strips, you need allow only an inch or two extra length for trimming. These materials are not washable, so consider this when placing them in a much-trafficked room.

The paper backing on which these materials are mounted can be weakened from oversoaking with paste. It is recommended, therefore, that the wall first be covered with blank stock to help absorb moisture from the paste. If you decide not to use

Trim edges of grass cloth.

FLOCKS

Flock is made of nylon or rayon and is available on paper, vinyl, or foil wallpapers. It presents no special preparation problems. It is fairly durable but can be damaged and flattened by rubbing and pressure. Therefore, use a paint roller or squeegee (available from your wallpaper dealer) rather than a smoothing brush to smooth it on the wall. Do not use a seam roller on seams, edges, or ends. Instead, pat down edges with a damp sponge or cloth, or use a new soft paint roller.

After hanging a strip, wipe in a downward direction with a damp sponge. Then, with a clean damp sponge, fluff up all flock with upward strokes to lay all nap in the same direction. Some small fibers will come loose during this operation, but this is no cause for concern.

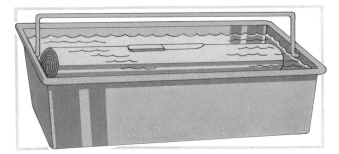

Weight paper down in water tray.

cut and soaked in water according to manufacturer's directions. Weight the paper down with a butter knife or other dull object to hold it under the water and to facilitate unrolling it. After soaking, it is ready to be hung.

No special surface preparation is required when using prepasted wallpaper—just make sure the subsurface is sound, smooth, and clean.

Wipe flock downward with damp sponge.

Wipe upward to raise nap.

PREPASTED WALLPAPER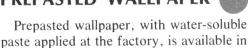

Prepasted wallpaper, with water-soluble paste applied at the factory, is available in vinyl and paper materials. The wallpaper is

PAPERHANGING TOOLS

In order to hang wallpaper properly, you need certain tools. Some of these, like an old table or sharp razor knife, you probably already have on hand. The other items are generally inexpensive and can be purchased at your wallpaper dealer's shop. If you have a rickety old stepladder, plan on purchasing a new one (see CHAPTER 4). Nothing is more annoying, or more easily preventable, than to have your wallpapering project interrupted by broken bones resulting from a fall off a broken ladder. At best you will end up on the floor wrapped like a mummy in sticky wallpaper. Avoid accidents by planning ahead.

A pasting table or other flat, hard surface at least 6 feet long is needed for cutting and pasting wallpaper. It can be rented, or you can make one by placing a sheet of ½-inch plywood on two or three sawhorses.

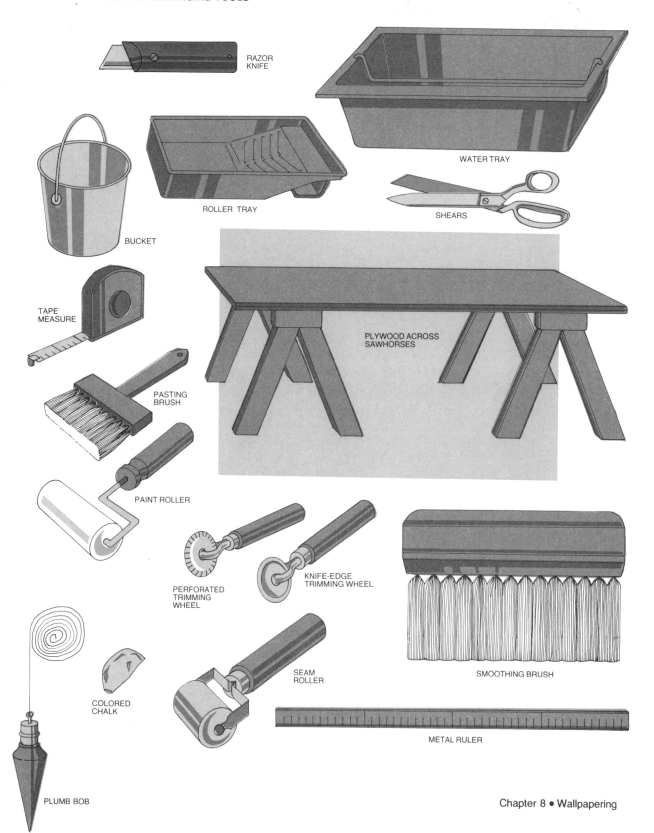

RAZOR KNIFE

WATER TRAY

ROLLER TRAY

SHEARS

BUCKET

TAPE MEASURE

PLYWOOD ACROSS SAWHORSES

PASTING BRUSH

PAINT ROLLER

PERFORATED TRIMMING WHEEL

KNIFE-EDGE TRIMMING WHEEL

SMOOTHING BRUSH

COLORED CHALK

SEAM ROLLER

METAL RULER

PLUMB BOB

Chapter 8 • Wallpapering

Two buckets, pails, or roller trays—one for paste, one for clear water—are needed. (If you're using prepasted wallpaper, just get one water tray.) A pasting brush, calcimine brush, or paint roller is necessary to apply paste if unpasted wallpaper is used.

Use a flexible metal tape rule to measure wallpaper lengths and widths, and a trimming knife to cut wallpaper. This can be either a sharp knife or a razor blade and holder. You should also have a trimming wheel to cut paper along baseboards or trim after it is installed. Two kinds, the perforated wheel and the knife-edge wheel, are available. A straightedge is essential for cutting straight lines. A long metal ruler is best, but any long, straight object will do. A chalk line will provide a true, straight, vertical guideline. You can make one with a piece of string, some colored chalk and a plumb bob or any object suitable for a weight.

A smoothing brush is used to smooth wallpaper against a wall and to remove air bubbles and wrinkles. The brush should be 12 inches wide, with bristles that are firm but soft enough not to scratch the wallpaper. (On some types of wallpaper, a soft paint roller is the preferred tool for the smoothing process.)

Shears or other heavy-duty scissors can cut wet wallpaper easier than a knife can. A seam roller makes tight joints at seams and edges. Use drop cloths to protect floors and furniture not removed from the room.

GENERAL PREPARATION OF WALL SURFACES

If old wallpaper is still in good condition, you can paper right over it. Any loose sections should be removed and the edges feathered with sandpaper. If the paper is generally loose, remove it completely with

Remove loose sections of old paper.

Feather edges with sandpaper.

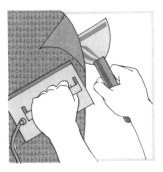

Removing old paper with steamer.

Removing old paper with chemical remover.

a rented steamer (following the renter's directions) or by soaking with wallpaper remover (following label directions). Where plaster is crumbling, scrape it away and patch with spackling compound, then sand smooth, as described in CHAPTER 5.

If you're papering over a low-gloss paint finish, dirt, grease, and wax must be removed. Following the label directions, mix a solution of trisodium phospate (TSP) to wash soiled surfaces. This provides a fine receptive surface for any adhesive.

If the surface paint is a shiny, high-gloss type, wallpaper may not stick well to it. This condition can be corrected by scrubbing with a solution of TSP or by applying a commercial deglosser. Consult a paint dealer for materials and recommendations.

If the surface is not painted, it must be sealed before applying sizing. Apply an oil-base sealer to unpainted surfaces such as new wallboard, plywood, or plaster.

It is generally advised to size surfaces before papering them. Sizing further seals the surface, preventing it from absorbing water from the wallpaper paste or glue, and thus allowing these substances to dry properly. (Vinyl adhesive should be used as sizing for nonporous wall coverings such as vinyl and foils.) Sizing also provides a roughened surface to which wallpaper paste can stick firmly.

For "breathing" wallpapers, you can use either of two sizing substances. Wallpaper paste, mixed according to manufacturer's instructions, acts as a sizing agent when applied to a surface and allowed to dry. Special wallpaper sizing is formulated specifically for this job.

Brush or roll a thin coat of sizing on the walls and allow it to dry. If the sizing turns pink in any area, it indicates a "hot spot" in the plaster; neutralize this area with a solution of zinc sulfate and water. Let dry and apply more sizing.

Take down all removable hardware that may be in your way. This includes cover plates for electrical switches and outlets and light fixtures. Since you will have to turn off the power in the room to remove the fixtures, you may find it convenient to do so only at the time you are actually papering around them.

Also remove curtain rods and brackets, drapery rods and brackets, and picture hooks. Screw holes will be difficult to find after they are covered with wallpaper. To save time and avoid having to drill new holes, place a toothpick in each hole. Remove the toothpick when papering over the hole, then push the toothpick through the paper back into the hole before going on to the next strip.

Apply sealer.

Apply sizing.

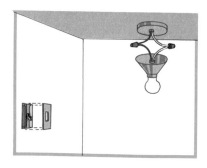

Remove wall plates, fixtures (left).

Put toothpicks in screw holes (below left).

Push toothpicks through wall paper (below).

PREPARING THE WORK AREA

A few minutes spent in organizing the paperhanging area will save time, mess, and tempers. An empty room makes the best work area. However, it is seldom practical to empty the entire room. Move out what furniture you can, and move the rest away from your work area so that you have as much room as possible for the ladder and for handling strips of pasted paper. Trying to work in a cramped space is both frustrating and irritating.

Bring all tools and supplies you will need into the work area. Set up a pasting table far enough from the surfaces to be wallpapered so as not to be in the way. Cover the pasting table with clean, plain paper such as freezer paper or brown wrapping paper. Never use newsprint to cover a pasting table; the newspaper ink is likely to soil the wallpaper.

REMOVING SELVAGE

Most wallpaper today is pretrimmed. The manufacturer has mechanically cut the edges so that strips can be butted together at a seam without the need for selvage removal. (Selvage is a narrow, unprinted strip on one or both edges of a roll of wallpaper.) A few smaller companies that produce specialty wallpapers still sell their products with the selvage intact.

The removal of selvage can be a time-consuming task. You should not be dissuaded, however, from buying a roll with these margins. The time required to remove the selvage will be well worth it if the paper is appealing.

Often, selvage strips are perforated for easy removal. In this case, simply strike the selvage sharply against a hard surface while turning the roll of wallpaper. The selvage will be torn off without damaging the patterned part of the paper.

If the selvage is not perforated, it must be cut off. It can sometimes be removed by the wallpaper dealer with a special tool. If the dealer cannot do it, you must remove it yourself. It is easiest to remove the selvage before cutting the wallpaper rolls into strips. Then, when you start hanging wallpaper, this work is out of the way.

To remove selvage, unroll some wallpaper onto your table. Align a straightedge with the selvage. Using a sharp knife, cut off the selvage. Roll the trimmed paper up so the roll looks like a scroll, one side trimmed and the other untrimmed. Repeat this process on the rest of the paper until all selvage is removed. Be careful not to damage flock surfaces by rubbing or pressing hard with the straightedge.

PATTERN LOCATION

Before cutting the first strip, determine where the pattern should end at the ceiling. This is a matter both of pattern and personal preference. Obviously, a pattern with human figures should not end with the heads cut off or just feet showing at the ceiling.

It is also important to remember that the line formed where the wall meets the ceiling is probably uneven. On painted walls, this unevenness often goes unnoticed. However, you may choose wallpaper with a pattern that forms a strong horizontal

Cut off perforated selvage and roll up trimmed paper, continuing to trim it.

Keep horizontal lines away from ceiling to make the uneveness less visible.

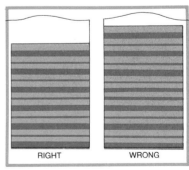

line. If this line is located near the ceiling line, the ceiling may appear noticeably uneven and the wallpaper poorly matched. Therefore, locate horizontal lines of a pattern as far as possible away from the ceiling line.

HANGING WALLPAPER

Follow the manufacturer's directions carefully when mixing wallpaper paste. Stir thoroughly until the mixture is entirely free of lumps. The paste should brush on smoothly, yet be thick enough to permit sliding the paper for positioning on the wall. If the manufacturer's suggested proportions result in too thin a paste, add a small amount of the dry powder to the mix.

If all four walls are to be papered, there will almost certainly be one place where the pattern cannot be matched. You should plan to locate this mismatch in the least noticeable place in the room. The best place for the mismatch is usually the least noticeable corner. However, sometimes a door opening or built-in cupboards or bookshelves can make a break in the pattern so that a mismatch will not be noticeable.

As a general rule, you should begin papering on the wall which is most noticeable and end in the corner which is least noticeable (or at another area, as noted above). After placing the first strip of wallpaper on the wall, work from right or left to the least noticeable corner. Then work from the op-

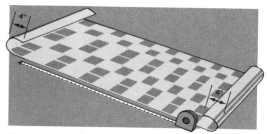
Measure and add 4 inches at top and bottom.

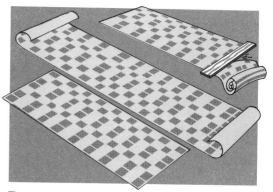
Then tear off the strip of wallpaper and tear off second strip to match first.

posite direction to the least noticeable corner or other mismatch location.

After locating where your first strip will go, hold a partially unrolled roll of wallpaper against the wall at the ceiling joint and decide where you want the pattern to "break" at the ceiling line. Mark this point lightly with a pencil and place the roll on the table. Starting at your pencil mark, measure off the distance from ceiling to baseboard.

Add about 4 inches above your ceiling mark and another 4 inches at the base for a trim margin, then tear off the strip of wallpaper, using a yardstick or other straightedge as a guide.

Lay the roll beside the first strip, unroll, and match its pattern to the pattern on the first strip. Tear the second strip off even with the first. Place it on top of the first, pattern up. Repeat this procedure with three or four more matching strips.

Mark the pattern break at the ceiling line.

Chapter 8 • Wallpapering

Apply paste to first strip.

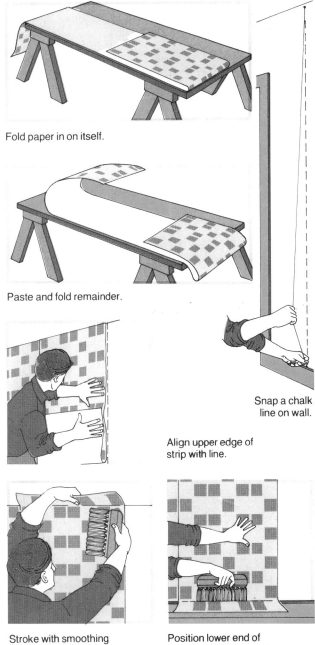

Fold paper in on itself.

Paste and fold remainder.

Snap a chalk line on wall.

Align upper edge of strip with line.

Stroke with smoothing brush to hold it.

Position lower end of strip, smooth with brush.

Now turn the pile of strips over, pattern side down, and push it back to the end of your work table. Take the first strip off the pile and line it up with the edge of the table nearest you. Apply paste to about two-thirds of the top of the strip.

Now fold the section in on itself—paste to paste. Align the edges of the strip carefully, but do not crease the fold. Paste and fold the remainder of the strip—again, paste to paste.

If you are using prepasted wallpaper, simply dip the strip into the water tank. Fold the strip over as described above and proceed to the next step.

The first strip must be perfectly vertical. This is important, as this strip serves as the placement reference for the entire wall. If you are starting in a corner, measure off a distance from the wall equal to one inch less than the width of the wallpaper strip. This extra inch will allow you to trim away the excess that may not be even because of the unevenness of the corner. Place a tack near the ceiling at the point you measured.

Chalk a plumb line and suspend it from the tack, allowing the weight to swing free. When it stops moving, hold the chalked line taut; pull it out at the middle and snap it against the wall.

Open the longer folded section of the pasted strip and position it at the ceiling. Align the outer edge with your chalk guideline, then give the upper area of the strip a few strokes with the smoothing brush to hold it. (For certain types of materials, as noted earlier, just press into place—do not use the smoothing brush.)

Unfold the shorter folded section and

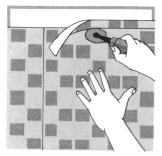

Trim at top.

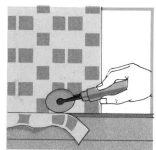

Trim at bottom.

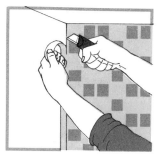

Trim at corner.

Press seams.

MAKING SEAMS

Butt joints have become almost the only method used for making seams between strips of wallpaper. They are by far the least noticeable of joints. A butt joint is made by moving the strip being hung against the strip already in place. Firmly slide the new strip tightly against the preceding one until a tiny ridge rises at the seam. As the paste dries, the wallpaper shrinks, causing the ridge to flatten.

Hairline joints are used only for blank stock, which is applied to the wall before hanging certain types of papers. A hairline joint is made by moving the strip being hung until its edge touches the edge of the strip already hung. As the paste dries, the paper shrinks, leaving a small hairline gap between the edges. This is invisible when the wallpaper is installed.

Lap joints, once common, are rarely used for seams between strips of wallpaper. They are noticeable and unattractive on an open wall. Lap joints may be used to make seams at corners. They are also used when small pieces must be joined together, such as fitting small strips in a casement window.

Do not use overlapping joints when hanging vinyl paper. Pastes made for vinyl do

guide it gently into place, keeping it on the chalk line. When this section is in position, brush from the center to the edges in sweeping strokes over the entire piece. Trim at top and bottom with a razor, a sharp knife, or, preferably, a wheel trimmer, then trim at the corner where necessary. Succeeding strips are hung in the same manner and in the same order in which they were cut.

After the strips have hung for 10 to 15 minutes, press the seams lightly with a seam roller. In the case of embossed or flock papers, seams are not rolled. With these wallpapers, a soft cloth pressed along the seams will serve the same end, while not crushing the flock or embossed pattern.

Remove any excess paste promptly from pattern, woodwork, etc. If the paper is a water-resistant type, wipe down the entire strip with a wet sponge. Use a clean, dry cloth on nonwashable paper.

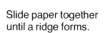

Slide paper together until a ridge forms.

Paper shrinks to form tight joint.

Chapter 8 • Wallpapering

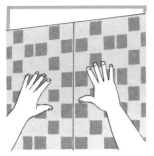

Hairline joint on blank stock.

Lap joint.

Making a double-cut seam.

not have strong adhesion for vinyl on vinyl. When hanging vinyl, use the double-cut seam method.

In this technique, a double cut is made at seams where the wallpaper strips have been overlapped. The cutting stroke must be firm enough to cut through both layers of paper. To make the cut, place a straightedge along the center of the overlap. With one stroke of the trimming knife, cut through both layers of wallpaper. Remove the trimmed strip from the top piece of wallpaper. Carefully pull the top wallpaper from the wall until the cutaway strip of the bottom strip can be removed. Then rearrange the seam, and smooth it down.

CORNERS

Special care should be taken when papering an outside corner. Do not rub on the paper where it passes around the corner. The surface of the wallpaper could be damaged.

Outside corners are more noticeable than inside corners. Mismatches are far more apparent at outside corners. Because of this, seams at or near the corner should be avoided whenever possible.

To paper around an outside corner, align the corner strip with the preceding strip. Cut a slit in the 4-inch trim margins at top and bottom and wrap the strip around the corner. Trim off the excess and let set. As

Lift top paper to remove cutaway strip below.

Smooth the seam after having it rearranged.

the paste dries, the strip will be pulled tightly against the wall.

Usually, papering inside corners results in some mismatch between strips. If the strips are carefully aligned, however, the mismatch will not be very noticeable. The correct way to paper an inside corner is to

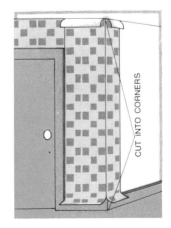

CUT INTO CORNERS

Papering an outside corner.

1. Measure distance between strip and inside corner.

2. Hang first strip in corner.

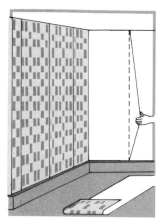

3. Measure second strip and snap chalk line.

4. Hang second strip.

tween the preceding strip and the inside corner at three different points up and down the wall. Add ½ inch to the greatest distance. Measure out the same distance on a strip of wallpaper and cut the strip to this width with a straightedge.

You now have two strips. The strip cut to the measurement arrived at in the previous paragraph is hung first. Measure and record the second strip's width. Beginning at the corner, measure out and mark this distance onto the wall to be papered. Snap a chalk line at this point. Align the second strip with the line. Some mismatch may occur with this method, but it will not be very noticeable, especially with smaller patterns. Remember: this overlapped seam will have to be double-cut if you are working with vinyl material.

PAPERING AROUND DOORS AND WINDOWS

The procedure for paperhanging around doors and windows is essentially the same. The first strip to be hung around a window

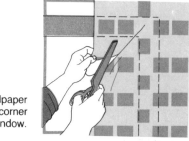

1. Cut wallpaper at top corner of window.

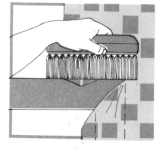

2. Smooth paper into joint.

cut the strip into two parts and overlap them at the corner. Never simply fold a strip and then paste it into a corner. It may pull away from the corner when it dries, becoming unsightly and subject to damage.

Measure and record the distances be-is aligned with the previous strip. The new strip is then pressed against the wall until it reaches the window. Don't press the top and bottom edges, however, until all cuts around the window have been made.

Using a smoothing brush (or paint roller), gently press the wallpaper into place where the wall and vertical edge of the frame meet. Cut the wallpaper at the top corner at a 45-degree angle into the outside corner of the frame. Using the smoothing brush, smooth the paper gently into place where the wall and top horizontal edge of the window frame meet. At the bottom corner, cut a 45-degree angle into the paper toward the lower outside corner of the window frame. Gently tap the wallpaper into place where the wall and bottom horizontal edge of the frame meet. Trim excess paper from around the vertical edge of the frame. Smooth the paper to the wall.

If more than one strip is required to paper around the window, repeat this procedure with the other side. The only difference between this process and papering around doors is that you needn't trim any bottom corners on door openings.

3. Cut wallpaper at bottom corner of window.

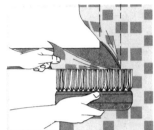

4. Press paper into place.

5. Trim excess paper around window.

9

Paneling

PANELING OF WOOD and other materials is versatile, easily applied, decorative, and utilitarian. It is excellent for new construction, remodeling, and redecorating. It can be had in hundreds of combinations of materials, styles, textures, colors, and finishes that will enhance the appearance and usefulness of any room.

Paneling prices cover a wide range, from about 10¢ to $10 per square foot. Paneling usually comes in standard sheets of 4 by 8 feet or, sometimes, 4 by 7 feet. This varies, however, and some types are available in plank form with a 16-inch width and a length of 8 feet. Most types on the market today have a factory-applied finish.

Prefinished paneling is usually far easier to care for than wallpaper or a painted surface because of its durability. It won't chip, crack, or peel as most paints will over a period of years. Nor will it rip or fade like many types of wallpaper. Depending on the type of paneling used, it will retain its original appearance indefinitely and require a minimum of maintenance. An occasional wiping with a damp cloth is usually enough.

One of the most important advantages that paneling offers the economy-minded, short-on-time do-it-yourselfer is its ease of installation. Unlike paperhanging or painting, very little mess is involved. Whereas you would have to clear most of the furniture out of the room before painting or wallpapering, with paneling you just have to push the furniture out of your immediate way, then push it back as you progress.

The few tools required, basically a hammer, saw, rule, and level, are found in most homeowners' tool kits anyway, so there's no need to purchase any special devices. You may have to make a few tricky cuts with a jigsaw or compass saw, depending on the shapes involved in your room, but the installation is simple enough for any weekend handyman or woman. The matching molding available with most paneling effectively hides any small blunders that may happen during installation (even the professionals make these "miscalculations").

The consumer should be cautious when purchasing paneling and know exactly what he or she wants before throwing any hard-earned dollars into the project. Measure exactly how much you will need, keeping in mind the dimensions of the individual pieces of paneling. You most likely don't want to have a patchwork-quilt effect on your walls, which is often the result when one overestimates the dimensions of paneling sheets and thus has to fill a small space with an odd-sized piece. The paneling simply won't stretch.

After completing your measurements, buy a little more than you need in case any panels become damaged or marred during installation. Also, since paneling styles are constantly being updated and discontinued, it is a good idea to keep some spare pieces around the house for repairs or add-on pieces for future projects.

Make sure your paneling is either flame-resistant or flame-retardant. Tragedies have resulted from the use of highly flammable housing materials. Many local building codes stipulate that all paneling used in a house must meet certain minimum fire safety standards. Even if your town or city has no such ordinance, it is wise to look for safety seals when choosing any building materials. Most major paneling manufacturers so rate their products; steer clear of those that do not.

Try to deal with an established, reputable dealer when purchasing paneling. Most good businesses stand behind everything they sell and offer you helpful tips on installation. Also try to stick with the name-brand paneling manufacturers. These companies generally guarantee their products, as long as they are installed according to directions.

TYPES OF PANELING

The do-it-yourselfer is faced with a pleasant dilemma once the walls and partitions of a home or addition have been framed and the insulation is put up, or when it is time to remodel an existing room. What type of paneling will be used? With the almost endless varieties and styles available, there is bound to be a pattern that exactly fits any designing plan.

Paneling materials are divided into three basic categories: hardboard, plywood, and hardwood-plywood. Hardboard is made from cellulose-based materials pressed under extreme pressure and then cut into planks or panels. A durable finish is added on one side. It can be purchased in thicknesses of ⅛ inch and ¼ inch.

Plastic-coated hardboard panels are a popular form of prefinished wall covering. The very strong bonded plastic finish withstands plenty of punishment and is easily maintained; a damp cloth will remove just about any dirt that hasn't been ground into the finish.

This type of paneling is available in many styles, textures, and colors. Wood finishes that simulate anything from Alpine oak to sable walnut are available. The graining and coloration of these panels make it hard to distinguish them from real wood surfaces. Most come with V grooves that divide the 4-foot-wide panels seemingly into planks of uniform or random widths. One type has slots in the V grooves so that shelves can be hung without nailing or any fuss. Matching moldings and shelving are available with this paneling.

Wood-grain paneling also comes in varying textures. Distressed wood designs like

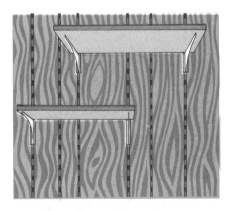

Slots in V-grooves of panels to support shelf brackets.

Brick-patterned
hardboard paneling.

Plywood paneling.

barnsiding and intricately sculptured designs like panels from the Byzantine period are included in this category.

Designer planks come in various colors and patterns. Finishes range from high-gloss to satin-gloss. Some have mural or mosaic effects. The wide variety of patterns puts this type of paneling in solid competition with wallpaper.

"Masonry" paneling simulates brickwork, stone, and stucco. Some of these come in tilelike segments that the do-it-yourselfer can nail or glue to the wall. After fastening, a calking compound is put in the grooves to give a grout effect and hide nailheads.

Suffice it to say that, whatever you can imagine in a wall finish, it has probably been done in hardboard paneling. With all the different types, installation is usually the same (with the exception of some of the masonry patterns in which "bricks" may interlock).

Plywood paneling is made of thin layers of wood joined together with an outer veneer layer of high quality. Most of it comes prefinished. Some varieties require the installer to do the finishing, but unless you are experienced in this type of endeavor, it's better to stick with the prefinished models. The cost savings are minimal with unfinished types, and usually the factory finish will far surpass your efforts in durability and attractiveness. The panels have a more natural appearance than the hardboard wood grains, and rightly so, because they are made from actual wood.

Hardwood-plywood paneling is essentially a spin-off of the above, using specially chosen hardwood veneers. The woods range in price and quality from relatively inexpensive Philippine lauan to a very elegant (and costly) Brazilian rosewood. With the very expensive panelings, the prices are dependent on the thickness as well as the species of the wood.

There are other forms of paneling, too. Although less popular than the hardboard and plywood varieties, fiberglass paneling is attractive and versatile. It is usually textured and requires professional installation. Fire-retardant and flexible, the panels can be bent to follow the curve in a ceiling or archway. Although more expensive than most hardboard paneling, fiberglass "masonry" patterns are very realistic and offer substantial savings over actual stonework.

Solid wood paneling, somewhat the vogue in past years, has drastically declined in popularity since the advent of fine-looking, easy to handle and install, and less expensive prefinished hardboard and plywood paneling. It offers very little in the way of fire safety, compared to the newer paneling. For these reasons, solid wood paneling is not recommended for home use.

TOOLS NEEDED FOR THE JOB

You can probably do the whole paneling installation with tools you have on hand. It would be wise, though, to replace saws or hammers that have seen better days. Good tools last for many years and are inexpensive in the long run. Savings in wasted materials alone generally more than offset the slight additional cost of better-quality tools. Keep your cutting tools clean and sharp, and protect edges and faces when not in use. Store them carefully.

Use handsaws or time-saving power saws on paneling, whichever you prefer. If you use a handsaw, make sure it is the cross-cut type. A ripsaw will generally chip the face of the paneling. Keep the panel face up when cutting so that the saw cuts into the face on the downstroke. Start cutting carefully at the panel's edge and support the cut-off material during final saw strokes so that it doesn't break off.

For circular power saws, a combination hollow-ground blade is recommended. With a table saw, keep the paneling face up while cutting. If you use either a portable power saw or a radial arm saw, make sure the panel is face down while sawing. Whether you use a handsaw or a power saw, put masking tape along the line to be cut. This will help prevent edge splinters and chips.

You may need a compass or coping saw or a jigsaw (saber saw) to help you get around tricky corners and odd shapes. A level and plumb line will keep your paneling on a true line throughout the room. A drill and a chisel will be helpful for cuts within the panel's perimeter, such as one needed to accommodate a light switch. You should have a claw hammer for driving nails and a rubber mallet for pounding panels into place and setting them in adhesive. If you don't have a rubber mallet, you can make do by hitting a 2 x 4 placed over the paneling (protected by a rag) with a claw hammer. This will distribute the blow evenly without damaging the paneling.

If you're putting the paneling up with nails, use a nailset with 3d (1¼-inch) finishing nails. (Some types of paneling come supplied with color-head nails to match.) A plane may be needed to even off old door

Crosscut handsaw.

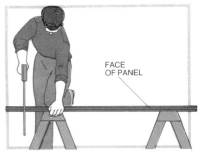
Cutting with a handsaw.

Cutting with a table saw.

Cutting with a radial saw.

Cutting with a portable power saw.

Compass saw, coping saw (top).

Put masking tape along line to be cut.

Saber saw.

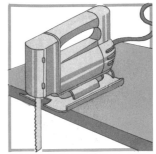

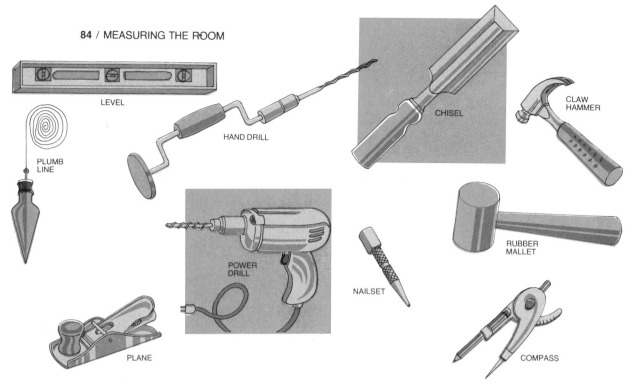

LEVEL

PLUMB LINE

HAND DRILL

CHISEL

CLAW HAMMER

POWER DRILL

NAILSET

RUBBER MALLET

PLANE

COMPASS

and window frames before paneling is installed over them. An art compass will be helpful in scribing out tricky or odd corners on the paneling.

MEASURING THE ROOM

Measure the length of all the walls, add these together, and the result will be the running length of paneling needed. In a room measuring 16 by 20 feet, the amount of paneling needed would be 72 lineal feet. If the paneling you have chosen comes in 4-foot widths, divide this dimension by 4 to find the number of panels required for the job—in this case, 18 panels.

Cutouts made for large openings (doorways, arches, windows) can often be used to panel under and over windows, for instance, or at stairways. You can estimate this use of otherwise wasted material by measuring carefully and, where possible, by planning to position a panel exactly at the edge of the opening.

As a double check, show your measurements and a sketch of your room layout to your dealer. He'll be glad to help and offer suggestions. Some types of paneling can be specially ordered in 10-foot lengths, suitable for older homes and apartments with very high ceilings. You may find, however, that the extra two feet will cost you substantially more than an additional 25 percent above the 8-foot panel's price. If this is the case, you might want to consider some other methods that will allow you to cover a 10-foot-high wall with 8-foot paneling. These methods are discussed later.

PANELING IN NEW CONSTRUCTION

If you're installing paneling in new construction, the preparation required is minimal and the problems that might arise are few. There are no old moldings in the way, for one thing. You have a chance to construct closets and built-ins with proportions

Number of Panels Needed
(Based on 8-Foot Ceiling Height)

Length of Room	Width of Room														
	6'	7'	8'	9'	10'	11'	12'	13'	14'	15'	16'	17'	18'	19'	20'
8'	7	8	8	9	9	10	10	11	11	12	12	13	13	14	14
9'	8	8	9	9	10	10	11	11	12	12	13	13	14	14	15
10'	8	9	9	10	10	11	11	12	12	13	13	14	14	15	15
11'	9	9	10	10	11	11	12	12	13	13	14	14	15	15	16
12'	9	10	10	11	11	12	12	13	13	14	14	15	15	16	16
13'	10	10	11	11	12	12	13	13	14	14	15	15	16	16	17
14'	10	11	11	12	12	13	13	14	14	15	15	16	16	17	17
15'	11	11	12	12	13	13	14	14	15	15	16	16	17	17	18
16'	11	12	12	13	13	14	14	15	15	16	16	17	17	18	18
17'	12	12	13	13	14	14	15	15	16	16	17	17	18	18	19
18'	12	13	13	14	14	15	15	16	16	17	17	18	18	19	19
19'	13	13	14	14	15	15	16	16	17	17	18	18	19	19	20
20'	13	14	14	15	15	16	16	17	17	18	18	19	19	20	20

that are easy to panel around, for another. In paneling a new room, you're building out from relatively straight, true walls.

With new construction, the heavier grades of paneling can be installed directly to smooth studs without furring. Use a wood plane to smooth imperfections, or shim out low spots if studs aren't perfectly straight. Building paper, plastic sheeting, or other vapor barrier installed against studs on outside walls will protect the paneling from moisture.

PANELING IN EXISTING CONSTRUCTION

Frame walls are normally constructed of 2 x 4 studs (verticals) and plates (horizontals) at floor and ceiling, to which the wall covering material (such as lath and plaster or gypsumboard) is fastened. Studs are set every 16 inches (center to center) and at door and window openings, where they are doubled. You must locate these studs if you

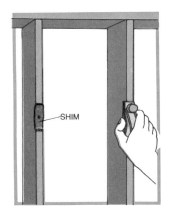

Correcting uneven stud surfaces with wood plane (at right) or shim out (at left).

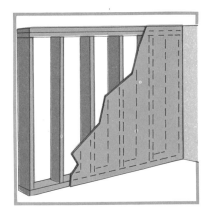

Stud finder.

Frame wall construction.

Tear out damaged plaster
and build out wall.

Nail loose wallboard
flat and tight.

Remove moldings with pry bar
before putting up paneling.

Drive finishing nails
through moldings.

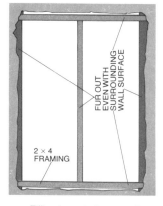

FUR OUT
EVEN WITH
SURROUNDING
WALL SURFACE

2 × 4
FRAMING

Filling in a window opening.

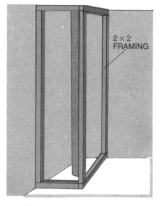

2 × 2
FRAMING

Frame around obstructions.

can purchase a magnetic stud finder in any hardware store. The wood stud won't attract the magnetic indicator, of course, but nails driven into it to attach lath or gypsumboard will.

If the existing wall is in good shape and solidly attached, you may be able to glue the new paneling directly to it or nail through the plaster or wallboard into the studs. If there is a small area of loose plaster, you can tear out that section and build it out with furring or plywood flush with the surface of the solid part of the wall. Loose wallboard can be nailed flat and tight. Paneling will hide many minor wall defects—no need to be too fussy. Just be certain that the defect won't get worse, to spoil your paneling efforts sometime in the future.

It's best to remove moldings before you put up the paneling. Do this carefully to avoid splitting, using a chisel or carpenter's pry bar. Or you can drive the narrow-headed finish nails right through the moldings with a hammer and nailset.

If you are filling in an opening, such as where you removed a door or window, build a stud framing and fur it out or cover it with wallboard or plywood to match the vertical plane of the rest of the wall.

Build a simple box frame around exposed pipes or other obstructions that you don't want to relocate. Paneling will decorate almost anything. If you're planning builtins—closets, wall shelving, cabinets—it's best to frame them out before you start to panel.

ARE THE WALLS EVEN?

Paneling can readily be installed on any dry nonmasonry wall that is in good shape, but other methods are needed when a wall is uneven. Check walls carefully for flatness. An uneven wall may appear even when painted, but it will look very obviously out of kilter when paneled over. This is

are furring the wall for paneling or nailing the paneling over the existing wall. To do this, tap the wall with your fist. A hollow thump means a space between studs; a solid sound indicates a stud location. Nailheads that show in baseboards or gypsumboard also indicate stud locations. Or you

Check for vertical and horizontal straightness of walls.

tions are noticeably large, compensatory measures will have to be taken before paneling is installed.

FURRING

One way to combat the problem of wall deviations is with furring strips. If the paneling is thick enough not to require backing (usually ¼ inch), furring is an easy and economical solution.

Furring strips may be nailed over the old wall, directly into the studs. If the existing wall is sturdy and solid, furring strips may also be fastened with adhesive. Follow label instructions for a secure bond.

Use 1 x 2 or 1 x 3 furring strips, or cut 2-inch-wide strips from sheets of ⅝-inch sheathing plywood. Space strips every 16 inches (measure from center of one strip to center of the next). Install either horizontally or vertically, following paneling manufacturer's recommendations.

especially true when the paneling utilizes straight lines in its design.

An easy way to check for wall straightness is to hold a room-height length of straight 2 x 4 lumber against the wall. If the board is flush with the wall at all points, then the wall is vertically straight in that area. Repeat this process, holding the board horizontally, to check for horizontal straightness.

There are other ways of determining vertical straightness and true perpendicularity. You can use a 2-foot carpenter's level or, better yet, a 4-foot bricklayer's level. Hold the level, lengthwise up, against the wall. As with the 2 x 4 method, if the level is flush with the wall, the wall is vertically straight in that area. If the bubble is not centered in the level, however, the wall is not perfectly plumb, or perpendicular with the ground level.

A plumb line can be used for this, too. Attach the line to the ceiling with masking tape at about two inches from the wall. With a ruler, measure the distance between wall and plumb line at different points on the line. If the distances are equal, the wall is both vertically straight and plumb.

It is very rare, even in new construction, for walls to be perfectly straight and plumb. If the walls are slightly off, paneling can usually be applied directly to them with satisfactory results. If, however, the devia-

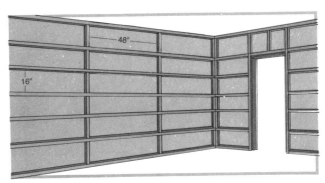

Furring strips over old wall.

Apply additional furring at doors, windows, etc. Don't skimp—use extra furring when in doubt. Where necessary, shim out furring to establish even planes, both horizontal and vertical. Pieces of shingle are ideal for shims. On an uneven wall take special pains to provide a firm, even base for the paneling.

BACKING FOR PANELING

When using thinner paneling, you may want to use gypsumboard as a backing (the alternative would be horizontal as well as vertical furring). In addition to its being an easily installed backing surface, it can also provide an appreciable amount of sound insulation in rooms.

Other similarly strong backings, such as plywood, particleboard, and fiberboard, could also be used for these purposes. Installation for all forms of backing is essentially the same. Gypsum wallboard, however, is the cheapest and the easiest to cut and install. Simply score both faces with a razor knife and break it off, then nail it to the studs.

Special annular-ringed nails are used for attaching gypsum wallboard. Make sure the nailheads are either flush with the board's surface or beneath it, keeping it perfectly flat so that paneling can be laid flush.

Don't forget the primary reason for using the wallboard, either. It is there to provide a perfectly flat, true surface for panel mounting. If you are nailing it over a substantial deviation in either the plaster wall or exposed studs, compensate for this.

PANEL PREPARATION

Certain measures must be taken before you put the paneling on the wall to ensure its adjustment to the room's climate.

Have the paneling delivered a few days before it is to be used. Do not store or install it in a room or building that has been freshly plastered or where humidity is high.

Be sure that the room humidity is about normal before applying the paneling.

Unpack it at least 48 hours before it is to be applied and flat-stack it with narrow strips of wood between the sheets, or distribute it around the room so that air can reach all sides of each panel. This will permit balancing of the moisture content of the paneling with that of the air in the room.

If moisture or excessive humidity may be a problem during some seasons of the year, back-treat plywood and wood-base paneling as recommended by the manufacturer. A good practice is to brush-coat a water-repellent preservative containing 5 percent pentachlorophenol, followed 24 hours later with a coat of sealer—aluminum paint for wood; shellac, varnish, or similar material for hardboard.

If there are differences in grain and color of the paneling, distribute it along the wall and arrange the boards or sheets to get the most attractive combinations. Number the panels on the back or with a removable marking to identify the sequence for application.

Nail a temporary, level strip of wood at the bottom of the area that is to be paneled. The bottom end or edge of the paneling can be set on it, and you will be sure that the panels will be plumb.

INSTALLING THE PANELING

It is generally easier to start putting up the paneling in a corner or at the end of an area. This provides a good frame of refer-

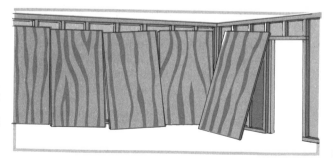

Line up paneling for best appearance (right); nail a leveling strip at bottom (far right).

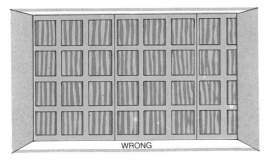

WRONG

For some patterns, start in middle of wall.

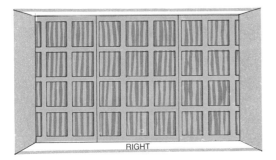

RIGHT

Tongue-and-groove and lapped edges make it possible to hide the nails.

Countersink nails.   Fill holes with stick putty.

ence and means that only one side will have to be cut in order to fit into the wall's width. With some panel designs, however, such as boxes or repeating motifs, it would look better to have both ends of the wall appear symmetrical. For this reason, starting the installation in the middle would be best.

Accurate marking, measuring, sawing, and fitting are necessary for a satisfactory job. Use a compass, saber, or coping saw to cut irregular lines. A block plane, a rasp, and sandpaper are helpful for fitting and smoothing the edges. Plastic wood, colored stick putty, and other patching materials can be used to repair or fill mistakes that will not be covered by the trim.

Panels grooved to represent random-width boards generally have a groove at each 16-inch interval, which is the usual spacing for studs and furring strips. Thus, nailing can be done in the grooves to hide the nailheads. Some types of paneling have tongue-and-groove or overlapped edges, which make it possible to hide the nails in the joint.

Color-coated nails that match the paneling can be used without countersinking. Otherwise, use 3d finish nails, countersink

them, and fill the holes with a matching color of stick putty. The panels should be well nailed around all edges and to intermediate support studs or furring strips.

USING ADHESIVE

Contact cement can be applied to both surfaces (paneling and furring strips or backing) at points of joining together. The cement can be applied with a brush or a serrated or saw-toothed spreader. The cement should dry to a nontacky condition before

Apply contact cement.   Press panel in place.

Apply mastic to studs.

Apply mastic to back of panel.

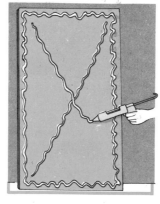

Nail close to ceiling; molding will cover them later.

Pull away from wall and block it out with scrap wood.

Tap to make contact.

Tap at joint.

few nails at the top and bottom of each panel with the adhesive to hold the paneling snug until the adhesive dries.

If you use a mastic adhesive for paneling over a backing, run a bead with a calking gun around the edges of the panel, and then make a big "X" in the middle. Turn the panel around and stick it in place. Be sure to butt it snugly against the adjoining panel and push it firmly into contact with the wall covering material.

When the panel is in place, drive a few nails along the top edge, close enough to the ceiling so that the molding will cover them later.

Pull the panel away from the wall and block it out with a piece of scrap wood. The nails at the top will keep it from sliding out of place. When the adhesive has dried for ten minutes or so, remove the block and press the panel into place. This step is necessary for a good adhesive bond.

Using a scrap of 2 x 4 for a buffer, hammer the surface of the panel lightly to make sure the adhesive makes contact over the entire surface.

Fit all joints snugly, but not too tightly. If paneling must be forced into place, put a scrap of paneling or board over the edges and tap lightly with a hammer.

When you come to an electrical outlet, make a pocket cut in the panel with a jigsaw to expose the outlet, or drill pilot holes and make the cut with a compass saw. To locate the area to cut away, measure from the floor and front edge of the previous panel to

the panels are set in place. Position the panels accurately before joining the coated surfaces—the panels cannot be moved after the coated surfaces make contact.

Another system uses a mastic-type adhesive that is applied to the studs, furring strips, or rigid backing material. A calking gun is used to apply it to studs and furring strips. Generally, it is necessary to use a

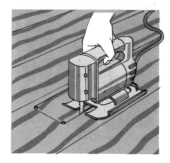

Pocket cut with saber saw for an electrical outlet.

the outlet. Transfer these measurements to the panel and make the pocket cut. To be safe and sure, measure twice, cut once. Another method is to chalk the outer edges of the electrical box, then press the panel in place against it, transferring the chalk marks to the back of the panel. The cut is then made as above.

When you have the panel attached to the wall, you can bring the outlet plug out flush with the surface of the panel by loosening the two screws that hold it in the outlet box. Replace the outlet cover with the center screw to cover the edges of the pocket cut.

As mentioned previously, some paneling is available in 10-foot lengths. Because of the expense or difficulty in finding your choice of paneling in this length, you may opt for the 8-foot length, even if your walls are higher than 8 feet. There are a couple of tricks for horizontally butting one piece of paneling to another while still retaining a good appearance.

One involves a "shadow line." The shadow line is a stripe of black painted on the

Paint black stripe on wall and install paneling to create "shadow line."

mounting surface behind the joint of the two pieces of paneling, usually at a point 8 feet below the ceiling. Then the panels are mounted about ½ to ¾ inch away from each other so that a "shadow" separates them. The shadow-line effect is especially pleasing with wood-grain paneling, less so with soft, pastel-colored paneling.

Another method of concealing a horizontal joint is to place the 8-foot section of paneling on the lower portion of the wall. A shelf is then installed 8 feet up the wall along the entire width. Another piece of paneling is put above the shelf and no one is the wiser.

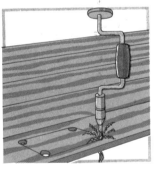

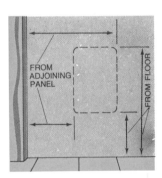

Drill pilot holes (far left).

Cut with compass saw (center).

Measuring to locate outlet (left).

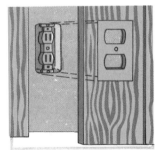

Chalk edges of electrical box (far left).

Press paneling against chalked edges (center).

Bring outlet flush with panel face (left).

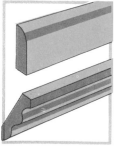
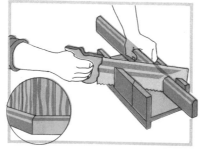

Base, ceiling moldings.   Mitering a molding.

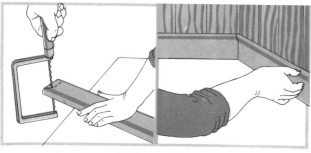

Coping a molding.

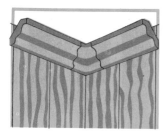

Outside corner molding (left).

Joining molding (below left).

Plastic joining molding (below).

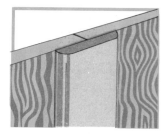
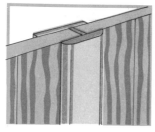

MOLDING AND TRIM

When all the panels are in place, nail molding at the ceiling line and nail on a matching baseboard molding. You can use finishing nails or nails colored to match the paneling for this job. Set colored nails flush with the surface; finishing nails should be countersunk and the holes filled with color stick putty to match the molding.

Where the moldings meet at the corners, you can either miter them (cut both at angles like a picture frame) or cope them (cut one molding to fit the curve of another). It's usually easier to miter outside corners (using a backsaw and miter box) and cope inside corners (using a coping saw).

In addition to ceiling and baseboard moldings, there are many kinds of moldings you can use to bail yourself out of tough fitting problems. Where panels meet at corners, you can use either wood or plastic moldings to make up for any slight discrepancies in fit. Outside corner moldings hide the edges of the panels and make tough wearing surfaces for the inevitable rough treatment an outside corner gets. You can butt panels together with a joining molding to hide any rough edges resulting from cutting a panel to fit a space narrower than the standard 4-foot width. With some types of plastic molding, you first put the molding on the wall with either nails or adhesive, then slide the edges of the paneling into it.

To fit paneling around windows and doorways, you should remove the trim molding and replace it to match the paneling. You can also install the paneling and nail the old molding back on. If you're really skilled, you can carefully cut the paneling to just fit up to the edge of a window or door molding, but this is a pretty tough job.

PANELING A BASEMENT

Installing paneling on a concrete or concrete-block basement wall involves a couple of extra steps, but it really is little more difficult than paneling any other room. The main difference is that you must put up furring strips (usually 1 x 2, 1 x 3, or 2 x 2 lumber) on the wall—you cannot apply the paneling directly. It is also a good idea to place insulation between the furring strips before applying the paneling, along with a vapor barrier. You may have to build a standard stud-frame wall to provide space for the insulation, depending on the type used. Your local building-supply dealer can help you with suggestions about what is best for your climate.

In many cases, especially on relatively new masonry walls, you can simply glue furring strips to the wall with special adhesive (again, consult your hardware or building-supply dealer). Glue horizontal strips along the ceiling and floor lines, then space vertical strips between them on 16-inch centers all around the room and in all corners. Check all strips with a level, and shim as necessary to plumb them.

Staple insulation between the furring strips. The store where you buy the insulation usually rents staple guns or hammers. Staple the insulation to the sides of the furring strips to leave the faces clear for applying the paneling.

If you need additional electrical outlets around the room, have the electrician install them before you start putting up the paneling. The outlet boxes should be flush with the surface of the paneling; special shallow boxes are available for this purpose. Make pocket cuts in the panels as explained above to accommodate the outlets.

To install the paneling, apply adhesive to the furring strips, rather than to the backs of the panels. Press the panels firmly into place as previously described.

To panel around basement windows, first glue a frame of furring strips around the window recess, flush with the front edge. Cut the paneling to fit up to the edge of the opening. Cut pieces of paneling to line the inside of the window recess and glue them in place. Use outside corner molding to cover exposed paneling edges.

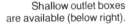

Glue furring strips to masonry walls (right).

Staple insulation (below).

Shallow outlet boxes are available (below right).

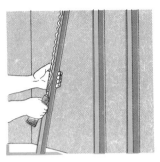

Apply adhesive to furring strips (left).

Glue frame of furring strips around basement window (below left).

Apply paneling and molding (below).

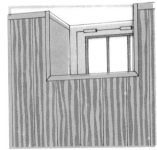

CARE AND MAINTENANCE

Wiping with a damp cloth is usually all that is needed to clean prefinished paneling when it becomes dirty. On some types, an occasional application of quality liquid wax

Fill large scratch
with sticky putty.

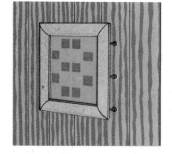

Holding picture frame
away from wall with nails.

is advised—follow the directions of both paneling and wax manufacturers.

Pencil and crayon marks and other heavily soiled areas may be cleaned with a mild soap or detergent. On plywood paneling, always wipe with the grain. After soil is removed, rinse and allow to dry thoroughly. Then (unless the manufacturer advises against it) apply a clear wax to restore the desired sheen. Cleansers that contain coarse abrasives are not recommended. Cleansers or waxes that leave deposits in the pores of wood should also not be used. On textured paneling, use heavy cloth wiping rags that will not catch on the raised areas of the design.

The finishes on modern plywood paneling are resistant to mars and scratches, but they do sometimes occur. They can generally be removed if they are in the finish only and have not penetrated into the wood. Use a clear wax on a damp cloth and rub the scratched area along the grain. You may have to wax the entire wall for a uniform appearance. But if the scratch goes through the finish and into the wood, a partial refinishing job will be required. Many scratches can be repaired with the use of a filler stick of the matching tone. If there is major damage, the services of a professional refinisher may be needed—or, if you were wise enough to purchase an extra panel or two when you first installed the walls, you might simply replace the damaged section.

Light has a tendency to mellow plywood wall paneling, except behind pictures, mirrors, and the like that are hung flat against the wall. This unevenness can be minimized by holding the picture or mirror out a bit—about a half inch—from the wall by means of nails placed in the backs of the frames. This allows light in behind the wall hanging so that the color tone mellows uniformly, leaving no sharp contrasts if the hanging is removed.

Low or fluctuating relative humidity can adversely affect any wood product. This is readily apparent when dry air causes a feeling of chilliness even when room temperature is 75 degrees or more. For your personal comfort as well as the health of the paneling, a humidity control system is recommended in high-humidity areas. With proper installation and care, your wall paneling will keep its good looks for years and years—a sound decorating investment.

Index